Praise
Love. Per

Rudy Rasmus is the real deal. Not only is he my friend, but he's a true Catalyst leader. His ministry and example have shaped and changed the lives of countless thousands of people in Houston and around the world. He's a shining example of *Love. Period.* We're all called to love, and Rudy shows us how.

—Brad Lomenick
author of *The Catalyst Leader*;
former President and Key Visionary, Catalyst

Rudy sees with God's vision: He sees assets where others see deficits. The principles of his life and his book are based on the simple but powerful premise that God's love radically changes lives.

—Dr. Kirbyjon Caldwell
Senior Pastor, Windsor Village United Methodist Church

Rudy is a pastor's pastor and a true inspiration. He lives a life dedicated to fully loving people, and this book will touch your heart to do the same.

—Leroy Barber
Global Executive Director, Word Made Flesh

In a neighborhood of folks our society has thrown away, Rudy Rasmus leads us to dispute the idea of expendable people. *Love. Period.* inspires and instructs us—especially the church—on how to love without conditions. If you really want to change the world, you must read this.

—Vance P. Ross
Senior Pastor, Gordon Memorial United Methodist Church

In *Love. Period.* Pastor Rudy Rasmus does something fresh and timely—he pulls back the curtain on all the ways love has been malformed in today's world, exposing many of our notions of love as frauds, and highlights on center stage the simplicity of love's essence. Resisting worn-out clichés, Pastor Rudy presses into the heart of the matter: that love loves for the sake of love. This book offers a much-needed invitation to be shaped by love in its purest essence. Not only challenging, but compelling and timely, *Love. Period.* will no doubt inspire you to live and love with a new sense of freedom!

—Christopher L. Heuertz
Founding Partner of Gravity,
a Center for Contemplative Activism; author of
Unexpected Gifts: Discovering the Way of Community

There is one word, one theological concept, one command that is the essence of the Christian faith. My friend Rudy Rasmus has written one of the most compelling books I've ever read about this word. Through story and insight he'll inspire you to pursue the "most excellent way."

—Adam Hamilton
Senior Pastor, United Methodist
Church of the Resurrection;
author of *Making Sense of the Bible*

After reading this book you will never think of love the same way. Rudy calls us to a Love Revolution where we love without conditions. The love Rudy describes is what we all long for, it's what the church desperately needs, and it's what the world is dying to see. It's revolutionary. It's transformational. It's love. Period.

—Shawn Casselberry
Executive Director, Mission Year

Rudy Rasmus

Love.Period.

When All Else Fails

WORTHY®
PUBLISHING

Published by Worthy Publishing, a division of Worthy Media, Inc., 134 Franklin Road, Suite 200, Brentwood, TN 37027.

HELPING PEOPLE EXPERIENCE THE HEART OF GOD

eBook available at www.worthypublishing.com

Rasmus, Rudy.
Love period / by Rudy Rasmus.
pages cm
1. Love—Religious aspects—Christianity. I. Title.
BV4639.R33 2014
241'.4—dc23

2013041133

Published in association with the Ted Squires Agency, tedsquires.com

For foreign and subsidiary rights, contact rights@worthypublishing.com

ISBN: 978-1-61795-215-9

Cover Design: Christopher Tobias, Tobias' Outerware for Books

Interior Design and Typesetting: Christopher D. Hudson & Associates, Inc.

Printed in the United States of America

14 15 16 17 VPI 8 7 6 5 4 3

For Juanita, a love supreme

Contents

Acknowledgments

Love. Period. has evolved out of my life's journey through sorrows and joys, valleys and plateaus, and from not believing in anything to believing that all things are possible through love. So, in many ways, this book is an accumulation of encounters with the best and worst that life has to offer—and realizing that it was never as bad as it could have been were it not for love.

To all of the people who have shown me love throughout my life, taught me the importance of love, and acted as examples of love, thank you. To all of the people who gave me a perspective on the importance of love by denying me love, withholding love from me, and by making a poor demonstration of the significance of love, thank you too. Every experience has been a learning experience on love.

My spiritual gift is "hanging out," and writing this book was really a community endeavor that evolved out of years of being with people on their journeys through life and love. If I started naming the beautiful souls who have touched my life I would miss the one person who has made the greatest impact. So to everyone who has cheered me on, encouraged, motivated, and believed in me . . . thank you!

I want to thank my friend and agent Ted Squires for always believing from the first book until now in the importance of my message on the power of unconditional love. Thank you also to the team at Worthy Publishing for taking a giant step with me to influence the world to love.

To my beautiful daughters, Morgan and Ryan, and my son-in-love, Hamilton, who have always been living reminders of the power of love, thank you.

Finally, to my wife, Juanita, whose life has been a window into the true meaning of what it means to *Love. Period.* Thank you for reminding me that *love never fails.*

A Love Revolution

Every one of us wants to be more than just accepted; we want to be loved. We all want to be loved fully and completely. Loved for who we are—regardless of our race, background, abilities, gender, economic status, identity, or physical condition.

Deep down, we long to be *loved. Period.*

When we consider what the Bible has to say about love, most of us think of the "love chapter" of the Bible. We have likely heard these words recited during a wedding ceremony or a sermon about marriage. So whenever we encounter 1 Corinthians 13, we tend to assume these principles apply only to romantic love.

But is the "love chapter" limited to a marriage relationship— or does this kind of love have a broader application for us?

Let's look carefully at the eloquent description of love that the apostle Paul gave to first-century Christians:

Love never gives up.
Love cares more for others than for self.
Love doesn't want what it doesn't have.
Love doesn't strut,
Doesn't have a swelled head,

Doesn't force itself on others,

Isn't always "me first,"

Doesn't fly off the handle,

Doesn't keep score of the sins of others,

Doesn't revel when others grovel,

Takes pleasure in the flowering of truth,

Puts up with anything,

Trusts God always,

Always looks for the best,

Never looks back,

But keeps going to the end. (1 Corinthians 13:4–7)

What an ideal! Just think of it: a selfless, sacrificing love that never quits, never keeps score, never becomes jealous, never seeks revenge, but just "keeps going to the end." Wouldn't you like to be loved in that way?

Want to know something amazing? This kind of love isn't just for romantic relationships. Not at all! This love is for regular people in everyday life. It's for you and for me.

"Wait a minute," you may be saying. "That sounds too good to be true . . . too perfect to be real."

What if I told you that it is absolutely possible, right now, for you to experience this kind of love? It is!

The apostle Paul was anything but a starry-eyed romantic or philosophical idealist. When he wrote these words to the church, he fully expected everyone who read his letter to do exactly what he said. He knew that you and I can actually experience the kind of love described in the love chapter—and the only way to experience this love is by giving it to others.

You and I can actually experience the kind of love described in the love chapter—and the only way to experience this love is by giving it to others.

Love is both a feeling (noun) and a doing (verb). If you *feel* love, then you must *do* the loving thing. When you *do* the loving thing, then you *feel* more love. It's a beautiful, God-designed cycle.

God wants you and me to love others in the real world the precise way He prescribed in the love chapter of the Bible. The kind of love God wants us to have and to receive—*love without conditions*—requires that we look outward as well as inward, and make sure both perspectives match up. Love is turning yourself inside out—to God and to others.

This book asks:

- What might happen if you and I took the words of the love chapter and began to apply them to our everyday lives?
- What might happen if we embraced the principles of 1 Corinthians 13 and used them as a pattern for all our personal relationships?
- What might happen if we began to move beyond our limited perspectives and truly considered the other person in every human encounter?

What a Love Revolution we might experience in our own hearts, minds, and souls!

The Most Daring Way to Punctuate Love

The love described in 1 Corinthians 13 is the most daring way we can ever experience life. As we have seen, it's not just love—it is *love without conditions*. This is the most liberating step we can take in building a dream, a sense of purpose, a vision, or a relationship.

To love without conditions is to say, "I choose to love. Period."

To love without conditions is to say, "I choose to love. Period."

The truth is, most of us love with conditions. We sometimes put a *comma* after our statement or vow of love. We slow down the flow of love ever so slightly so we might judge, assess, and evaluate.

- "I will love you, but I'll need some time to think about it."
- "I will love you, but I have to know more about you first."
- "I will love you, after I find out if you are a safe person."

At other times, we punctuate our love by adding an *if*, *when*, or *maybe*.

- "I will love you *if* you do . . . or say . . . or change in some way to make my love easier to give."

- "I will love *when* you do this—and not until."
- "*Maybe* I will be able to love again, or *maybe* I can continue to love, or *maybe* I can find it in my heart to love you. But maybe not."

Sometimes we place *question marks* after our vow to love because we are afraid of being disappointed, hurt, or rejected.

- "I think I will love you . . . at least, I'll try, all right?"
- "I will love you . . . but not fully, in case you hurt me or reject me, okay?"
- "I'll love you . . . but could you please give me some space to protect my heart so I'm not disappointed again?"

Sometimes we place *parentheses* around our love to shut off the rest of the world from seeing just how vulnerable we are feeling.

- "I will love you (as long as you don't ever find out about *this* part of me)."
- "I will love you (but you will never know that I have done *this*)."
- "I will love you (though I will never let you look deep inside my heart to see my true fears and feelings)."

Sometimes we place *dashes* in our statements of love to create detachment so that what seems like the foolishness of our love decision has no way of coming back to haunt us or to bring ridicule to us.

- "I will love you—from a safe distance."
- "I will love you—as long as I don't have to get too involved."
- "I will love you—on the condition that I don't have to make any sacrifices or be embarrassed by being seen with you."

However, an entirely different reality sets in when we put a period after our decision to love.

- "I will love you. Period."

When we say, "I choose to *love. Period*," we are signaling to the world that a revolution has taken place in our hearts. All the conditions of love have been rolled away like the stone from Jesus' grave, and we are ready to see what God might do—in us and though us—with His unending, ever-powerful, life-giving, reconciliation-producing, restoration-accomplishing love.

Putting a period after our love says we have closed all the escape hatches and we are willing to risk all possibilities of disappointment, heartbreak, and loss in our desire to see what God might do with our faith and love to work His miracles through us.

Putting a period after love is a reminder to all who see or hear us that Jesus has unlimited capacity to love and that He was not simply a prophet with a few good ideas; rather, Jesus is the ultimate source of love for all people, of all ages, under all conditions, for all time. It was out of *love without conditions* that Jesus came to this earth, died on the cross, and rose again.

Jesus is the ultimate source of love for all people, of all ages, under all conditions, for all time.

When we put a period after our love, we send a signal to all negative forces in the world that we choose to set no boundaries on God's ability to defeat the manipulative bullies of the universe.

The period after our love is a rallying cry that says a new order is now in place in our lives and we refuse to be intimidated by race, class, gender, orientation, past deeds, or any other limitation that squelches potential or possibilities.

Love. Period. That's what indicates we have decided to trust God no matter what—and we believe with our whole heart that love will triumph over evil!

What Would Happen?

Just imagine what would happen if somehow the church started putting a period after our love and became ground zero for a Love Revolution. Do we care enough for it to happen?

When something *revolves,* it turns completely around from where it was, to a different perspective. Whether the revolution is social, institutional, or technological, all revolutions start when people recognize that something needs to be turned or changed. A revolution is a drastic, far-reaching way of thinking or behaving that is different than the norm.

The church desperately needs a Love Revolution today.

**The church desperately needs
a Love Revolution today.**

Consider this: Jesus was a young revolutionary who was misunderstood by the established religion, which was a big business. Jesus preached a message that included game-changing concepts like creating economic and social equity and deconstructing gender bias. Jesus was a Love Revolutionary who demonstrated authentic healing, challenged the extortion taking place in the temple courtyard, and ultimately offered people freedom from the religious elitists who were controlling their everyday life.

The frustrated religious elitists said about Jesus:

This man keeps on doing things, creating God-signs. If
we let him go on, pretty soon everyone will be believing
in him and the Romans will come and remove what
little power and privilege we still have. (John 11:47–48)

A Love Revolutionary is someone who looks at the existing structures and says no to the prevailing system because he or she can no longer live and breathe within an absence of love. A person who loves without conditions responds, "This structure and authority doesn't make sense without love." Jesus truly was a Love Revolutionary.

Insurgents are people who see problems with the existing structures and do one of two things: walk away or demand change. Today's insurgents either leave the church—which they are doing in record numbers—or they loudly and forcefully demand that the church become the institution its founding document, the Bible, says it is.

But there is a third, more powerful, alternative in responding to today's existing systems. Instead of being an insurgent, I urge you to join me in becoming a Love Revolutionary.

Imagine what would happen if we united in spreading a Love Revolution, starting in the church and moving out to our communities and the entire world! With unconditional love as our primary motivation, we could change broken systems so that people all over the world will experience real love.

Responding . . .

1. "Love is both a feeling (noun) and a doing (verb). If you *feel* love, then you must *do* the loving thing. When you *do* the loving thing, then you *feel* more love. It's a beautiful, God-designed cycle." Respond to these statements. Do you agree? Disagree? Why?

2. How do you punctuate your love? Does your love come with commas? Qualifiers? Question marks? Parentheses? Dashes? Describe why you are punctuating love the way you are.

3. Are you an insurgent—a person who either walks away or makes demands—or are you willing to help change

broken systems with the unconditional love of a Love Revolutionary?

4. In what ways would your life and relationships be different if you decided to *love. Period*?

CHAPTER 1

Love Is Diverse, but Not Divided

When I was nine years old, I made a deeply committed vow that I would protect my family from all danger—seen and unseen. That vow shaped my life for the next thirty-six years.

My vow formed my perspective on relationships. It fueled my anger against perceived injustice for many years. It shaped my thoughts on mercy and love. It significantly affected my life as a hustler-turned-pastor who ultimately became a Love Revolutionary.

What did my childhood vow have to do with my faith and with the reality of a God who loves without conditions? In a word . . . *everything.* My vow to do whatever it took to protect my family resulted in anger toward anyone who could hurt us and ultimately became the lens through which I processed life— my own identity, the value of others around me, and all definitions related to character issues, including whether something or someone was worthy of love.

A World with Two Fountains

I grew up in a world of two water fountains. One was marked "Whites Only." The other said "Coloreds Only." Having two fountains when one would suffice baffled me as a child. I asked my mother about it more than once: "What's different about the water that comes from the 'Whites Only' fountain?" She would reply, "Nothing. But you better not ever drink from it."

As I grew older, I began to understand what those two fountains meant. I learned that the world judged the worth of people based on the color of their skin. Even in Sunday school, I found it difficult to comprehend why God, who controlled everything, would allow a world to function with such deep separation between people on the basis of color.

**I learned that the world judged
the worth of people based on
the color of their skin.**

Why couldn't black people sit in certain sections of the bus or in all areas of a restaurant? Why did black people have to go to special restrooms in public places? Why couldn't we drink from the same water fountain as everyone else?

Racism Gets Personal

During my early childhood, racism was mostly a peripheral experience for me. I had seen examples of it, but I had not yet experienced the deep humiliation of being directly confronted by it. Then, in the summer of my ninth year, I went shopping with my mother and Aunt Norma in downtown Houston. My aunt had just finished her freshman year in college. I was excited to spend the day with Aunt Norma because she was close enough to my age to not quite be considered a grownup. She was a cool aunt. She didn't let things bother her, and everyone seemed to like her. When I was with Aunt Norma, I felt like everything was okay.

After the three of us went to several stores together, Mom split from us and told us to meet her at the bus stop later. Aunt Norma took me to a few other stores and then we found the bus stop in front of Wolf's Pharmacy. That particular pharmacy had an old-fashioned soda fountain where you could get a milkshake while waiting for the pharmacist to fill a prescription. Aunt Norma decided to treat me to a soda.

I followed her into Wolf's and up to the counter. There weren't many people in the store, so Aunt Norma sat down on one of the empty stools at the counter. I sat down next to her and watched her scan the menu on the wall and then tell me my options. Mr. Wolf walked over to us, a bit flustered, and said, "No. You can't sit here." He waved his hand at us as if we were flies and motioned to a back room secluded from the main part of the store. "You have to sit back there."

Aunt Norma's mouth dropped open, and for a moment, I thought she was going to shout at him in anger. Instead, she silently took my hand and led me out of the store. "Just keep walking," she told me. We walked past the bus stop and on to the store where my mother had said she was going to shop. Aunt Norma told Mom what happened at the pharmacy, and my mother replied, "You shouldn't have done it."

Aunt Norma was part of a generation of young men and women who were angry at the status quo and weren't willing to sit by and let race be a dividing factor anymore. My mother was part of a generation that accepted the status quo and tried to make peace and continue with life, doing good where good could be done.

I am part of a generation that seems to think racial discrimination is a thing of the past . . . but I know it isn't.

I am part of a generation that seems to think racial discrimination is a thing of the past . . . but I know it isn't.

A Two-Way Street

Some time ago, I had a conversation with a friend who is a white man serving as a choir leader. In his career, he has worked in both predominantly black and predominantly white churches. He explained his opinion of why white people don't generally attend churches led by black pastors: "They're unfamiliar with the music and style of worship, and they're unable to interpret the cultural nuances and the sermon's style. It's difficult when they don't know what to do, so they don't try." He went on to tell me that he sometimes felt racism as a white man serving in a black church—he felt he was not wanted.

I was saddened when he said that. I wanted to disagree. But I know he was speaking the truth of his experience. I don't *want* it to be the reality that racial discrimination still exists, even in the church. And I don't *want* it to be the reality that racism is a two-way street, at least to some degree. But it is so.

The critical issue is, how are we to respond to racism?

**The critical issue is,
how are we to respond to racism?**

My response at age nine was to make a vow that I would be a defender against any injustice that might harm me or my family. It was not a decision to hate whites—or to hate anybody, for that matter. But neither was it a decision to extend love to anybody.

First Corinthians 13:1 says, "If I speak with the tongues of men and of angels, but do have not love, I have become a noisy gong or a clanging cymbal" (NASB). I didn't protest loudly with outrage at racial injustice. In my heart, however, I was blotting out strong, positive messages of love, compassion, concern, and bridge building with any people beyond my neighborhood. These impulses were in my spirit, but my defensive heart could not hear them over the noisy gongs of apprehension, fear, mistrust, and disillusionment.

I didn't join marches or carry signs or go on angry looting rampages. I simply built an emotional wall that separated me from others and chose to stay behind it, dancing there to the clanging cymbals of "safe" separatism.

I wasn't doing anything to rile up racial tension. I simply refused to cross the racial divide. I had adopted the position: "You stay on your side and I'll stay on my side—and don't try to cross over to my side or you'll be confronting a young warrior who will defend his family to the death."

I wasn't doing anything bad or hateful. But I also wasn't doing anything good or loving.

Confronting the Fears That Divide

I believe that fear is at the heart of racism. In truth, fear is what separates us from most people we perceive as being different. Yet the apostle John wrote, "There is no room in love for fear. Well-formed love banishes fear. Since fear is crippling, a fearful life—fear of death, fear of judgment—is one not yet fully formed in love" (1 John 4:18).

**Fear is what separates us
from most people we
perceive as being different.**

I saw this kind of well-formed, fearless love in my Auntie Mae Mae's store. Auntie Mae Mae treated everyone who walked through the door of her neighborhood grocery store as if he or she was the most important person in the world. She wasn't afraid of people who looked strange, smelled bad, or acted weird. She pushed aside the fears that others seemed to have and showed love to everybody, all the time.

If you have been allowing your fear to keep you from loving others without conditions, I challenge you to take the following action steps, starting today:

- Admit that you are afraid of people who are different from you.
- Feel the vulnerability that comes with the thought of allowing the stranger into your space.
- Act as though fear cannot keep you from loving.
- Step out in courage to love. Period.

Love Builds Bridges over Fear

I believe that if you actively seek to love—no matter what—you *can* build bridges with people over any chasm of fear.

"Why bother?" you may be asking.

The answer is twofold. First and foremost, Jesus told us to love others and to do so without fear and without regard to external factors. He said, "Love your neighbor as well as you do yourself" (Luke 10:27). If we are truly going to follow Christ, we need to do what He told us to do.

Second, love is the most powerful force on the earth to bring healing to people's hearts and healing to broken communities. The Bible says, "Trust steadily in God, hope unswervingly, love extravagantly. *And the best of the three is love*" (1 Corinthians 13:13; emphasis added). Love is the power that brings about genuine change—from the inside out—that results in better neighborhoods, better churches, and better communities for all of us.

Hate destroys in obvious ways. Hate erupts in wars, rampages, vengeance, and violence. Apathy destroys just as effectively, but usually in far less obvious ways. We don't need to hate in order to see decay or decline. We simply need to do nothing— we simply need to close our hearts to love without conditions.

We don't need to hate in order to see decay or decline. We simply need to do nothing—we simply need to close our hearts to love without conditions.

My defensive posture as a nine-year-old stayed with me for decades. My vow to keep a position of separatism kept my eyes wide open and my heart closed tight. It stopped me from getting involved in a positive way in any kind of racial conflicts. And it prevented me from truly experiencing the freedom and strength that occurs when we take a proactive position that says, "I will show *love. Period.*"

Our God-Designed Differences

In order for us to take a strong pro-love position, we need to recognize that God built differences into humanity. We are not all alike. In fact, no two people are exactly the same in every dimension. We may have vast similarities, but we are not clones of one another.

In the Bible, the psalmist praises God for making him unique:

You shaped me first inside, then out;
  you formed me in my mother's womb.

I thank you, High God—you're breathtaking!

Body and soul, I am marvelously made!

I worship in adoration—what a creation!

You know me inside and out,

you know every bone in my body;

You know exactly how I was made, bit by bit,

how I was sculpted from nothing into something.

Like an open book, you watched me grow from

conception to birth;

all the stages of my life were spread out before

you. (Psalm 139:13–16)

We must recognize that God not only made each of us unique, but He had a specific design and plan in making us. God never seeks to wipe out our differences; rather, He calls us to champion our differences, unite our hearts, and then use our individual God-given talents and abilities in collaborative ways to solve problems and create solutions—even to problems we have not yet identified or defined!

The apostle Paul explained:

God's various gifts are handed out everywhere; but they all originate in God's Spirit. God's various ministries are carried out everywhere; but they all originate in God's Spirit. God's various expressions of power are in action everywhere; but God himself is behind it all. Each person is given something to do that shows who God is: Everyone gets in on it, everyone benefits. All kinds of things are handed out by the Spirit, and to all kinds of people! The variety is wonderful. (1 Corinthians 12:4–6)

We each have our own unique skills and gifts. We each have a specific cultural and racial dimension to our lives. We are diverse in our callings, our talents, and our ministries. What hinges us together as Christians is *not* clinging to our differences and defending them as valid. What melds us together into an active and effective body of Christ is our choosing to build bridges of love across our differences.

What melds us together into an active and effective body of Christ is our choosing to build bridges of love across our differences.

God designed us so that no one person can do everything or be everything. Only Jesus filled that role. He designed us to find ways to work together, minister together, worship together, and build together. The Bible urges us to "speak the truth in love, growing in every way more and more like Christ, who is the head of his body, the church. He makes the whole body fit together perfectly. As each part does its own special work, it helps the other parts grow, so that the whole body is healthy and growing and full of love" (Ephesians 4:15–16 NLT).

What is the glue that makes our joining together possible to all who choose to accept? God's love. It is His love, working in us and then through us, that enables each of us to "fit together perfectly . . . so that the whole body is healthy and growing and full of love." Being filled with God's love enables us to move beyond our defensive postures in life and to build relationships across all barriers and chasms that divide us.

**Being filled with God's love enables us . . .
to build relationships across all barriers
and chasms that divide us.**

A Third Fountain from the Mouth of the Lion

One of my favorite places to visit as a child was the Houston Zoo. I loved watching all the animals and spending time with my parents there. The highlight of any childhood trip to the zoo was the lion fountain.

From the gaping mouth of the lion statue, a stream of water gushed out into a shallow pool. Children were free to run around that fountain and have the time of their lives splashing in the pool on a hot day.

The beauty of the lion fountain was that there weren't any signs around it saying who could or couldn't play in its waters. This was not a fountain for whites. It wasn't a fountain for blacks . . . or Asians, or Hispanics, or Native Americans, or Semites, or any other race of people. It was a fountain for all people who simply desired to cool down on a hot day.

That's one of the best metaphors I know for the way God desires to see the church function. Jesus—the Lion of Judah— gave Himself to us so that we might partake fully of what gushes from Him: *love*. He delights when we all splash around together in His love. His love is the force that can cool down all the forces of anger, hatred, bitterness, resentment, pride, and all other negative emotions that heat up our world to a near-melting point.

God's love is a fountain for all people. His love is for everyone to drink in . . . and then share with others.

Responding . . .

1. Is your stance toward the world defensive or proactive? Are you seeking to protect or defend yourself and others from injustice—or are you seeking to be proactive to change injustice through acts of love?

2. Do you have a fear of a particular type of people you perceive as being different than you? If so, how does your fear divide or separate you from individuals who belong to the group you fear?

3. What are some specific steps you can take today to stop fearing this group of people and begin to show them *love. Period*?

CHAPTER 2

Love Has No Conditions

I have loved the circus since I was a kid. My mom would take me every year, and I could hardly sleep the night before in anticipation of what I was sure would be an afternoon of marvel, merriment, mystery, and miracles.

Under the big top, my mind would soar with the possibilities of the marvel of flying as I watched the trapeze artists sail through the air with the greatest of ease. I would laugh with the clowns and wonder how they could all fit in that little bitty car. I marveled at how they could have so much fun and merriment at their work.

At the circus, I ate food that I could only experience at the circus—for me, the concessions were like once-a-year manna. While I was at the circus, my eyes would become as wide as apples as I watched the fearless lion tamers and came to believe that people could actually communicate with these dangerous, wild animals.

Under the big top, I would gaze in wonder as people swallowed fire, exploded out of the mouth of a cannon without getting hurt, jumped safely from a tall tower onto the backs of other people, and flew through rings while riding on horses ten times their size.

When the circus tent was darkened, its ceiling would become a night sky filled with stars, all under the command of a ringmaster who orchestrated the mystery, marvel, and merriment.

Every year, I begged my mom to take us again to the circus—to see the same acts over and over. It was there, under the big top, that I discovered something greater than the show in the three rings on the sawdust floor. At the circus I experienced the miracle of being in a room filled with people of all races—everyone having fun without any of the racist problems associated with which drinking fountain or restroom a person was using. The atmosphere in the giant tent was filled with unrestrained love and acceptance for every person there. At the circus, I felt equal, desegregated, free, entertained, engaged, challenged, and loved unconditionally.

**The atmosphere in the giant tent
was filled with unrestrained love and acceptance
for every person there.**

I respected the ringmaster for guarding this culture of marvels, merriment, mystery, and miracles for a kid whose name he would never know—but a kid who needed the experience as desperately as he needed oxygen. I appreciated the ringmaster and all the people connected to the circus for bringing marvels, merriment, mystery, and miracles close enough for a kid like me to experience them. You see, at the circus, I felt love without conditions. I know my mama paid a price for me to experience it, but when I walked into that big tent I felt loved fully and completely.

It was the circus, more than any other event or environment, that shaped my view of the church. The question I asked myself then and am still answering is a simple one: "Why can't church be more like the circus?" Of course, I am not saying that the church should imitate the circus by using magic tricks and showmanship. I mean, why can't the church provide the ultimate in marvel, merriment, mystery, and miracles? Why can't the church always be a place of love without conditions?

Why can't the church always be a place of love without conditions?

I readily admit that, as a pastor, I take very seriously my opportunity to be the ringmaster of the sacred circus called church. I long for people to experience an amazing God who imparts unending joy and love. To me, the gospel of salvation through Jesus Christ is a *marvel*. And because of this amazing gift freely offered to everyone, *merriment* should be the norm at church. Jesus is synonymous with *mystery*—and His wonders never cease. At the core of it all, love is the real *miracle*.

At the circus, all conditions are stripped away so that love is given without conditions. The same should be true of church.

Don't Bury Your Love Behind Conditions

Removing the conditions! That's what love does. Love defies the conditions that keep it from doing its divine work. How do I know that? Because Jesus walked up to a tomb where the entrance was covered by a stone, and He refused to accept the conditions He found there.

When Jesus received a message that His friend Lazarus had become deathly ill, He waited a few days and then traveled to Lazarus's hometown of Bethany. Lazarus's sisters, Mary and Martha, were grieving and disappointed that Jesus hadn't come earlier to heal their brother. But Jesus knew something they didn't: He was going to raise Lazarus from the dead!

However, before Jesus could bring His friend Lazarus back to life, the stone that blocked the opening of the tomb had to be moved.

Look at how the apostle John describes the scene:

When Jesus finally got there, he found Lazarus already four days dead. Bethany was near Jerusalem, only a couple of miles away, and many of the Jews were visiting Martha and Mary, sympathizing with them over their brother. Martha heard Jesus was coming and went out to meet him. Mary remained in the house.

Martha said, "Master, if you'd been here, my brother wouldn't have died. Even now, I know that whatever you ask God he will give you."

Jesus said, "Your brother will be raised up."

Martha replied, "I know that he will be raised up in the resurrection at the end of time."

"You don't have to wait for the End. I am, right now, Resurrection and Life. The one who believes in me, even though he or she dies, will live. And everyone who lives believing in me does not ultimately die at all. Do you believe this?"

"Yes, Master. All along I have believed that you are the Messiah, the Son of God who comes into the world."

After saying this, she went to her sister Mary and whispered in her ear, "The Teacher is here and is asking for you."

The moment she heard that, she jumped up and ran out to him. Jesus had not yet entered the town but was still at the place where Martha had met him. When her sympathizing Jewish friends saw Mary run off, they followed her, thinking she was on her way to the tomb to weep there. Mary came to where Jesus was waiting and fell at his feet, saying, "Master, if only you had been here, my brother would not have died."

When Jesus saw her sobbing and the Jews with her sobbing, a deep anger welled up within him. He said, "Where did you put him?"

"Master, come and see," they said. Now Jesus wept.

The Jews said, "Look how deeply he loved him."

Others among them said, "Well, if he loved him so much, why didn't he do something to keep him from dying? After all, he opened the eyes of a blind man."

Then Jesus, the anger again welling up within him, arrived at the tomb. It was a simple cave in the hillside with a slab of stone laid against it. (John 11:20–39)

There is *always* a stone standing in the way of the power of love. There is a stone somewhere that is covering a dream . . . a desire . . . a calling of God . . . a purpose for good.

There is *always* a stone standing
in the way of the power of love.

Many of us have rolled a stone in front of our dreams to keep everyone out. We think we are avoiding hurt, frustration, and despair. In truth, we likely are turning away from our greatest nuggets of potential and hope!

Love Overcomes Any Condition

Tombs are the end of the line for unfulfilled dreams. They are the last stop for potential and promise. They represent the end of hope, the conclusion for all unfulfilled ideas. Tombs are the places where you find yourself mourning the loss of something you valued, in which you invested, for which you may have worked very hard.

Tombs say, in a very tangible way, *The End*.

Tombs are a fact of the natural world. They are the epitome of *conditions*. Consider the following conditions in the scene where Jesus has come to the tomb of Lazarus:

- There likely was a condition that caused Lazarus's death.
- There were conditions that surrounded his burial.
- There were conditions that kept the tomb sealed.

But Jesus—surrounded by a doubtful, suspicious crowd—spoke to the tomb in which Lazarus was buried. You see . . . Jesus knew something the crowd did not know, not even His closest and dearest followers in that crowd. He knew that love overcomes *all* things. When encapsulated in words of faith, love can even overcome death—yes, even after four days of death!

Let's go back and read the rest of the story, as told by the apostle John:

Jesus said, "Remove the stone."

The sister of the dead man, Martha, said, "Master, by this time there's a stench. He's been dead four days!"

Jesus looked her in the eye. "Didn't I tell you that if you believed, you would see the glory of God?"

Then, to the others, "Go ahead, take away the stone."

They removed the stone. Jesus raised his eyes to heaven and prayed, "Father, I'm grateful that you have listened to me. I know you always do listen, but on account of this crowd standing here I've spoken so that they might believe that you sent me."

Then he shouted, "Lazarus, come out!" And he came out, a cadaver, wrapped from head to toe, and with a kerchief over his face.

Jesus told them, "Unwrap him and let him loose." (John 11:39–44)

Love can overcome *any* condition that separates us from all that God has for us!

Love can overcome *any* condition that separates us from all that God has for us!

Roll Away the Stones That Block Your Love

Before Jesus called to Lazarus inside the tomb, He demanded that the stone be rolled away. Note clearly that Jesus did not roll the stone away by Himself; instead, He commanded the people there to roll it away.

And that is still the case. He is still asking you and me to roll away the stone of conditions that seal shut our dreams and our love for others.

The tombs that keep our dreams in death are sealed with a stone of conditions. The conditions might be anger, doubt, hostility, confusion, fear, bitterness, or lovelessness, or a combination of all these in varying degrees. The conditions might be prejudice, injustice, hate, or lack of faith.

Each of us must address the conditions we have placed on the death of our dreams and spiritually and mentally roll away those stones. We must be willing to experience the new power, new life, and expanded capacity to love that comes when we invite Jesus Himself into the scene.

Our freedom—and the new life of our dream—is as close as our willingness to love God and to love our neighbors as ourselves . . . *without conditions!*

**Our freedom—and the new life of our dream—
is as close as our willingness to love God and
to love our neighbors as ourselves . . .
*without conditions!***

The Extreme Power of Love

Without a doubt, God's love is powerful. It can restore us to life even when all indications are that we are lifeless. The stone that covered Lazarus's tomb is symbolic of our belief in the permanency of natural laws. In order to transcend the natural reality, the stone covering the tomb *had* to be rolled away.

The same is true in countless situations today. Something is dying or dead that God wants to be *alive!* But it is sealed in a tomb, usually of humans' making.

We must roll away the stone so God's love can do its work. And one thing is vital for us to use if we are to unseal a closed tomb—faith. We must *believe* God has called us to roll away the stone. We must *believe* that God has a life-producing work to do. We must *believe* God desires to manifest His love and for us to manifest His love imparted to us.

**We must roll away the stone
so God's love can do its work.**

Once the people rolled away the stone from the entrance to Lazarus's tomb, Jesus' love for His friend was allowed full opportunity to do its work. Jesus, in the midst of being surrounded by a doubtful, angry, suspicious crowd, spoke life into that lifeless tomb. His words—spoken from a heart of love and faith—were sufficient to bring *life!*

In our world today, tombs are a good metaphor of the end of the line for all unfulfilled dreams, unrealized potential, and unkept promises. Tombs represent the finality of hopes, the conclusion of ideas and plans. A tomb is the place you find yourself after others have given up on you and you have given up on yourself.

When Jesus' call came for Lazarus to "come forth!" (John 11:43 NKJV), only one person came out of the tomb—but many were set free by hearing and witnessing the miracle. Jesus brought life out of death, and life out of death is how Jesus' followers understood the kingdom of God after that momentous day. It is how we are to understand God's kingdom today.

The question is, will you and I hear and respond to Jesus' call to us, "Come forth"? Will we allow ourselves to be called out from the tombs of our own making and sealing? Tombs must never be regarded as the end of anything God blesses, desires, honors, or favors. The stone that seals a tomb must never be regarded as immovable.

Your freedom to pursue God's potential is closer than you can imagine! It is often as close as your willingness to love God and to love your neighbor as you love yourself (Matthew 22:37–39).

Love without Limits

John Dominic Crossan observed, "An action performed on one single body reaches out to become an action performed on society at large."[1] Imagine surgery being performed on your heart and simultaneously repairing the hearts around you. God is the surgeon, and love is the scalpel. When God wields His scalpel of love, He cuts away all anger, doubt, hostility, confusion, fear, bitterness, and lovelessness.

If you allowed God to remove the limits to your love, how would your life—and the lives of others around you—be different?

If you allowed God to remove the limits to your love, how would your life— and the lives of others around you—be different?

The love of Jesus has no end. It has no limits. It has no weaknesses, no fallibilities, no flaws, and no failures.

How will you love today?

How will you trust Jesus to love *through you* right now?

Responding . . .

1. Have you ever experienced the miracle of a changed attitude after seeing God perform a miracle in the life of another person? Describe what happened.

2. Are you open to the possibility that God might perform a miracle in your own life that could affect others around you in a highly favorable way? What might that miracle in your life look like?

3. In what ways are you open to . . .

   marvel—at your amazing salvation through Jesus Christ?

   merriment—in your relationship with Jesus?

   mystery—at God's wonders?

   miracles—that are produced by love?

CHAPTER 3

Love Replaces
Fear with Faith

Do you live in a place with good air?

If you can *see* the air where you live, the answer is probably no.

If there's nothing between you and a huge, bright blue canopy of sky dotted with white, puffy clouds, then the answer is a big, "Yes, the atmosphere here is good!"

Love is intended to be the big yes of our existence. Love is to be the atmosphere of our life—the clean, refreshing spiritual air we are to breathe as we live in Jesus and He lives in us.

Love is not intended to be bound to one particular event, experience, or behavior. It is not intended to be limited to one type of relationship, or one season of life. Love is for everyone at all times and everywhere. It is meant to be *love. Period.*

In this chapter, we will use the letters in the word *love* as an acronym to explore the atmosphere of love. Unpacking the acronym LOVE, we come up with this statement:

Love *liberates* us so we can walk fully in the truth of God's love, and reach out to *others* with great *vulnerability*, in order to *engage* others in a relationship that brings honor to God.

Let's examine each of these elements of LOVE more closely.

The L in LOVE Stands for Liberation

When are we given permission to stop loving God or loving others? *Never!* Jesus said that His entire teaching could be summed up in one simple statement: "Love the Lord your God with all your passion and prayer and muscle and intelligence—and . . . love your neighbor as well as you do yourself" (Luke 10:27).

Not sometimes. Not sporadically. Not with any qualifiers. We are to *love. Period.* And that means always.

To maintain a steady atmosphere of love around us means we must acknowledge what love does—in us and through us—and also how love works.

What does love *do?* It sets us free to be wholly the persons God designed us to be. Love allows us to be authentic and to function fully at the peak of all the talents, dreams, abilities, and attributes that God created in us. Love allows us to fulfill God's purposes for us.

Love allows us to fulfill God's purposes for us.

How does love do its work? It calls us again and again to the truth of God's love for us. *Truth* is the word we use when something conforms to reality or to provable facts. The truth is that God loves us, sent Jesus to love us, and continues to send the Holy Spirit to express love in us and through us. Truth is what sets us free to love. How? Because God loved us, we are empowered to love others. God's love is not only our example, but it is also the liberating force that sets us free to love without conditions.

If we are having trouble expressing love, feeling love, or pursuing love . . . then there is something blocking our freedom to love. It's like the flow of water through a pipe that is suddenly blocked by a rock that becomes wedged in the pipe. The one thing that can dislodge the rock and renew the flow of love is a strong reminder that we are to love *as we have been loved* and *as we are loved by God*. Our unconditional love for others comes from the wellspring of His love.

Our love has the potential to be unlimited, even revolutionary, if we will allow the flow of God's love to surge through our words, actions, and attitudes. As we remember that Christ died for us and rose from the dead for us, we are confronted with the liberating truth that Christ also died for the person who stands before us in need of love. We dare not withhold the love that God so freely and generously desires to show another person—*through us.*

**Our love has the potential to be unlimited,
even revolutionary, if we will allow
the flow of God's love to surge through
our words, actions, and attitudes.**

The O in LOVE Reminds Us of Others

Love requires that we reprioritize our concerns so that we factor in the needs of others. We are called to love others *as ourselves* (Luke 10:27). Not more than ourselves—and also not less than ourselves. The level of consideration we give to our own needs is the level of consideration we are to give to the needs of others. What we want for ourselves must become what we want for others. Love is never something we possess exclusively for our own selves. True love is intended to be manifested upward to God and outward to others, without hesitation and with huge amounts of generosity.

**True love is intended to be manifested
upward to God and outward to others,
without hesitation and with
huge amounts of generosity.**

I've concluded one thing about human interaction—it feels better if conversation is about positive *possibilities*. People enjoy talking about opportunities, the likelihood of a future good time, the spark of a perhaps-it-might-work relationship, or the excitement of an innovative idea. But when the possibilities are negative, or when there are no possibilities . . . there is no fun.

I think that one of the antonyms for the word *possibility* is *tradition*. Tradition tends to keep people stuck in the same old way of doing things and of relating to one another. That explains a lot about the atmosphere of many churches! Of course, not all church traditions are wrong or inherently negative. But some churches can become so steeped in tradition that they can't see any possibilities that might further human interaction or relationships. In churches that have adopted this kind of atmosphere, there doesn't seem to be much fun . . . and often, I suspect, not much love.

For love to flourish in any group, there must be a genuine appreciation for other people and opportunities to explore new relationships.

The V in LOVE Stands for Vulnerability

Many people try to avoid being vulnerable to others. Love, however, requires vulnerability. In fact, it requires that a person *embrace* vulnerability. Madeleine L'Engle once wrote, "When we were children, we used to think that when we were grown up we would no longer be vulnerable. But to grow up is to accept vulnerability. . . . To be alive is to be vulnerable."[1]

Vulnerability involves uncertainty, risk, and emotional exposure. Those who do *not* want to be vulnerable often crouch behind walls of inadequacy and insecurity, and the result in their lives is very often a scarcity of loving relationships.

Love requires a generous heart that is free of fear and a willingness to let yourself be known, even as you become willing to know others, including their unpleasant traits.

**Love requires a generous heart that is
free of fear and a willingness
to let yourself be known.**

The E in LOVE Reminds Us to Engage

We may be willing to be vulnerable, but if we don't actively reach out and *engage* in speaking to, interacting with, and acknowledging the importance of others . . . there will be no love.

The truth is, we are all involved with one another to some degree. We can't avoid it. When we attempt to deny that we are interdependent, we become brittle, isolated, lonely, and, often, depressed to the point of despair.

If you want to discover how a person loves, and in that discover the core of his character, you need to look at the fruit of his life. If he has abundant fruit that is rooted in caring, free-flowing communication with others, you are likely to find a person who is loving. Where there is no fruit of abiding, warm relationship, there is likely no engagement with others and very little love.

Fear Keeps Us From Living in LOVE

What keeps us from engaging others with vulnerability in order to free others, and ourselves, to live fully in God's love?

Fear.

Fear is the number-one, most longstanding factor that keeps us from reaching out to others. Dr. Martin Luther King Jr. spoke eloquently about fear. He said:

> Normal fear protects us; abnormal fear paralyzes us. Normal fear motivates us to improve our individual and collective welfare; abnormal fear constantly poisons and distorts our inner lives. Our problem is not to be rid of fear but rather to harness and master it.[2]

**Fear is the number-one, most longstanding
factor that keeps us from reaching out to others.**

Before we can fully engage with others, we usually need to confront one or more of our own deepest fears, some of which may have been acquired many decades ago. That has certainly been true in my life.

Our perception of the things we fear is often greatly exaggerated from reality. I have a fear of snakes. So if I see a four-inch snake, you just might find me describing my near-death encounter with a four-foot python! Fears seem to exaggerate themselves with almost no effort on our part.

In addition to my fear of snakes, I have also been afraid of many other things. One of those things was flying. I did not step foot on an airplane between 1988 and 1998 because of fear. I made excuses to avoid air travel. I faked illness to avoid travel. I even lied occasionally to keep from getting on a plane. After some time in therapy, I realized that my fear was not really about flying, but rather about lack of control. My need to control things originated in the unresolved issues of my childhood.

Many of our fears are developed during childhood. No person is truly born with fear—except perhaps the fear of falling (which we probably acquired when we fell out of the womb of our mother) and the fear associated with sudden loud noises (which we probably acquired when we found ourselves hearing with clarity the once-muffled noises of human voices and machinery in the bright environment of the hospital delivery room).

The truth is that most fears are *learned*, and many of those fears are learned in early childhood, when we are the most vulnerable and susceptible to environmental factors and to the people who have been charged with our care and safety. Never mind that the people in authority over us are likely learning their roles on the job. They have power over us, and we tend to learn to defend, protect, and pursue new possibilities according to *their* fears over what we can, should, and might be able to do.

The truth is that most fears are *learned*.

It's really no wonder that we live in an age of chronic anxiety—our society is aggressive, reactive, and in need of quick fixes with few assurances. Most of us are surrounded by chronic complainers and control freaks. As my wife often reminds me, "People control what they can."

Why are we like this? Because we have been taught that this world is a big, bad place filled with mean people who are out to take everything they can from us. And unfortunately, since the people who surround us have also been taught this same thing, the meanness and hatred and strong attempts at control continue . . . and escalate.

J. Keith Miller, in his book *Compelled to Control*, wrote that most of our fears are an attempt to conceal our true identity from others. We are afraid that if people know who we really are, what we really think, and what we are capable of doing, we will be rejected. And since we do not want to be alone, we "polish up our outer personages until we honestly believe they are the real us."[3]

Faith Is the Opposite of Fear

We all have fears that can keep us from loving without limits. Not long ago, I came across an A-to-Z list of phobias. I discovered there's a phobia for just about everything—from achluophobia (fear of darkness) to zemmiphobia (the fear of mole rats). It's amazing what we allow ourselves to fear—even when we have a basic understanding that phobias paralyze us, poison us, and distort our own self-perception.

How are we to address our fears?

Faith.

Faith is the opposite of fear. Faith doesn't deny the reality or presence of fear; rather, faith is the power to overcome fear. Faith gives us the ability to move forward in love in spite of our fears. That may be one of the reasons the Bible so often says, "Fear not!" As long as people are wrapped up in a cocoon of fear, they cannot experience the penetrating, healing power of God's love. He wants us to activate our faith so we might reach the potential He has for us!

Faith gives us the ability to move forward in love in spite of our fears.

Faith is *more powerful than fear.* That's one of the key things we must believe to the point of unshakable conviction.

God can do what we cannot—and His power is unlimited. It is accessed by *faith*.

God knows what we do not know—and His wisdom is unlimited. It is accessed by *faith*.

God is present at all times and is in control of all things—and His presence is accessed by *faith*.

We do not function in *our* faith. We function under the protective shield of Jesus' faith to do in us and through us what He desires to accomplish on this earth—which will always be for our eternal benefit and earthly blessing. He invites us to do revolutionary acts of faith to accomplish His purposes through us.

It's an amazing thing that God wants to use *your* faith and *my* faith in order to perform the great and mighty acts of love that can transform all of humanity!

Where Should We Aim Our Faith?

If we see our faith as the ultimate weapon against our fear—and then realize our faith is embedded in Jesus' unconquerable and unlimited faith—where should we aim our faith? At our greatest pain and deepest need!

Henri Nouwen wrote, "The dance of life finds its beginnings in grief. . . . Here a completely new way of living is revealed. It is the way in which pain can be embraced, not out of a desire to suffer, but in the knowledge that something new will be."[4]

What has caused you the greatest sorrow? What experience or relationship has created the greatest ongoing pain for you?

That's the place where *fear* has very likely taken strong root in you. And that's the place where *faith* needs to be aimed!

Never discount the trauma you've experienced. Don't try to run from it, cover it up, deny it, or turn away from it. You can learn incredible lessons from your heartaches and even find that God's purpose for you has been shaped by those events. C. S. Lewis once wrote, "Pain insists upon being attended to. God whispers to us in our pleasures, speaks in our consciences, but shouts in our pains. It is his megaphone to rouse a deaf world."[5]

You can learn incredible lessons from your heartaches and even find that God's purpose for you has been shaped by those events.

God uses pain to get our attention, and His purpose in doing so is a good purpose! He sets up our pain as the target for our faith so we might deepen our dependence on Him, move past our fears, and learn to *live in love*. When we experience God's love, we can lower our guard of self-protection, and we can love people without conditions.

The more we take aim at our fears—and the pain and sorrow associated with them—the more we find that faith truly does have power over fear. And in that realization of truth, we nearly always find that we can lower our guard of self-protection and truly begin to reach out to others—to engage them, to be vulnerable with them, and to *love* them.

Faith Releases Love
That Overcomes Fear

Avoiding pain is a natural human instinct. I would like to avoid the painful part of lesson learning, but the longer I live, the more I realize the inevitability of pain and pain's connection to our spiritual growth and our relationship with God.

Pain and its persistent sidekick, suffering, pave the road into our deeper selves.

**Pain and its persistent sidekick, suffering,
pave the road into our deeper selves.**

Each of us has painful potholes in the road we have walked in life. We have been hurt. We have been rejected. We have been victimized to some extent by someone at some time. We have been blindsided by a social suicide bomber or an emotional landmine. Nobody escapes pain in this life.

Not only is pain inevitable, but we have all developed a basic memory problem when it comes to pain. We simply don't want to remember our pain. We don't want to think about it, talk about it, or be reminded of it—because most of us don't have a way to keep the painful memory from hurting us again.

And that brings us back to faith! We stuff our pain into a shell with a hard surface and bury it somewhere. The call of love is to take a sledgehammer of faith to that hardened shell and not only break it open but defeat it by declaring, "Jesus loves me more than any situation . . . any experience . . . any abuse . . . or any trauma can hurt me! God's Word says that Jesus in me is greater than the forces of evil. God's Word says that the love of God heals, restores, and transforms my pain into a thing that brings blessing and glory! I choose to believe God's Word. It is a greater reality with greater power than my human-sized pain."

Faith releases the love that overcomes fear and heals the deepest wounds of fear. It empowers us to LOVE!

Responding . . .

1. Are you afraid of being "found out" by others? Are you afraid of being rejected by others? How do these fears impact your willingness to love others—to be vulnerable to them, or engage in relationship with them?

2. Has God ever used the megaphone of pain to get your attention? How did you respond? What did God do?

3. Do you believe that your faith in Jesus is greater than your greatest pain? Do you truly believe your faith is coupled in a lasting, unbreakable way with Jesus' faith? To what fear might you turn your faith?

4. In what ways do you struggle in your relationships? In what ways is LOVE compelling you to become more vulnerable, engage others more freely, and respond to others with faith rather than fear?

CHAPTER 4

Love Never Quits

I'll never forget the day I told my father that I would no longer work with him in our motel business. That brief statement changed everything about our relationship—in an instant.

Dad knew I wasn't just quitting a job. Far more was involved in my decision. The motel business was no longer who I was or what I was about. It didn't fit me anymore. It wasn't really about me—it was about God and what He was requiring of me.

My father responded with a look that cut to the very core of my soul. His expression went beyond disappointment; it signaled estrangement. Dad didn't say a word. He just turned away from me. It was several years before we experienced the closeness we'd always had up until that moment.

My Role Model

When I was a child, my dad was my role model. I will never forget the day when I was about nine years old, hanging out in the street with my friends in what was the closest thing we had to a baseball field. My friends and I were trying to decide who would be on which team.

In my old neighborhood, leadership was earned. Two boys who were the usual leaders assumed the roles of captain and began to call out the names of the players they wanted. From the most gifted to the least gifted, the names were called, and then only the scrubs were left. I was one of them. Finally I was the only one standing. One of the captains said, "All right, Rudy, you are on our team." There was no enthusiasm in his voice.

At that point, of course, I wanted to quit. I loved baseball, but I was so hurt and embarrassed by being chosen last that I didn't want to play anymore.

That afternoon, I went home and told my dad what had happened. Dad said, "Let's take a ride." And off we went to a nearby department store where Dad bought me a bat, a baseball, and a glove. When we got home, he took me out to the front yard so all the neighborhood kids could see me. He showed me how to hold the bat and how to swing it. He taught me to keep my eye on the ball as it came toward me and to step forward into the swing when the ball crossed the plate. In our neighborhood, it wasn't normal for a dad to take time out of a Saturday to play ball with his son. Slowly, a little crowd began gathering along the fence surrounding my front yard—the other kids were amazed at the rare sight of a father taking time to interact with his son. It was obvious that these boys wanted to be included. Dad leaned over and whispered, "You wanna be captain?"

Dad taught me that day that love never quits. Dad placed a high value on loyalty and perseverance. He used to say to me,

"I'm with you, riding or walking." That meant he would be with me regardless of the cost or consequences.

He didn't want me to quit playing neighborhood baseball in the face of ridicule or rejection. Instead, he called to the other boys to come inside the gate, and then he left me to become the captain of the game played in my own front yard.

Prior to that day, I hadn't felt as if I belonged. But that afternoon I became the captain. And the next day, the boys all asked me to be the captain again.

Love Accepts Unconditionally

Dad later taught me about business. He had a basic philosophy that was in keeping with what Jesus taught: if you treat people like you want to be treated, they'll generally respond with reciprocal treatment toward you. That may not sound revolutionary to you, but in my neighborhood—it was truly revolutionary!

When my father conducted business with customers at the motel we owned, he always talked straight with them. He never cheated anyone. He never turned away a customer on the basis of how he or she looked, dressed, or acted. Rich people did business with us, and so did poor people. In Dad's eyes, cash from one customer was as good as cash from another.

Unconditional acceptance is a concept that businesses understand. There are times, however, when it is a lesson that seems to have been lost in the church. Perhaps the church doesn't really understand the core concept that everybody is either a buyer or a seller. I learned that concept early—in my aunt's grocery store, in our motel, and in our other enterprises. We in the church are always to be *selling*—the power of Christ, the unique position Christ gives His followers, the responsibilities that come with His grace, and the love that He expects us to give freely.

Since I was raised with such a strong conviction about accepting unconditionally and *not* quitting, why did I decide to quit my job at the motel business?

A Time to Quit and a Reason to Stay

My dad had involved me in his motel business as the managing partner. The problem was that this motel was actually a borderline bordello. It was a place where prostitutes plied their trade with the men of Houston. We weren't pimps, and we didn't get a cut of the money the prostitutes made. We were innkeepers who simply provided a key to a room and changed the sheets and towels after those who paid for the room left. My father and I saw preachers, professional businessmen, and people of every walk of life come in for an hour or so with a "date."

The message to my dad, of course, was filled with discrepancies. Here were people who claimed to love others, but they would treat people like commodities. Here were people who claimed to have found a better way to live, but they were living in a way that used people and pulled people down to the lowest levels of morality.

After years of working with my father in the motel business, I was also a little jaded and a whole lot suspicious. But something had happened in my life that had set me on a path in a very different direction.

I had met Juanita, who became my wife. Juanita had led me to church, which eventually led me to Jesus. And ultimately, that encounter led me to a desire for a vocation in ministry.

My father was aware of this progression in my life, and when I told him that I was leaving the motel business, he was *angry*! It wasn't that I was quitting as much as *why* I was quitting. I was choosing the church over him.

Dad and I had been partners my entire life. We had been best friends. He had helped me out of a lot of situations—both financially and physically. I owed him my life. And now he perceived me as turning my back on him. He told his friends that he had "lost me to God."

At the time I announced to my father that I was leaving the motel business, Juanita and I had started working at St. John's United Methodist Church, in downtown Houston. Money was very tight. We had grown accustomed to a certain level of motel management income, and once that was gone, we were in trouble. We started falling behind on mortgage payments. Knowing that I had gone to my dad for help in the past, I figured he would probably help me again. I told him of the financial trouble my family and I were in, and I will never forget his response. Dad looked me straight in the eyes and said, "Go ask God."

Yes, the division between us was that deep. Dad didn't smile when he said it. His words weren't angry—but they cut like a razor because my father was making it very clear that he felt I had given up on him, and therefore, he was giving up on me.

His reaction could have made me bitter or angry. But I saw that this was a test of my faith. Yes, I *could* and *would* go to God with the problem and trust God for help. And yes, I *could* and *would* continue to love my father.

I learned a critical lesson: It is entirely possible to quit a job, an alliance, a position—and to continue to love a person and to stay in relationship with that person!

**It is entirely possible to quit a job,
an alliance, a position—and to continue
to love a person and to stay in relationship
with that person!**

We need to see our opportunities for loving relationship to be with one person, as opposed to a group of people. If we begin to love the group, we can sometimes lose sight of our need to distance ourselves from a group that is engaged in activities that are contrary to God's desires for us—and for those in the group!

Jesus said that we are to love our neighbor as ourselves. He didn't say we are to love the neighborhood. There's a very big difference.

There are times when God may lead a person to separate himself or herself from the gang . . . or from the club . . . or from the social set that goes to the lake on weekends . . . or from the group that vacations at the casinos. We are to love the people, but we may need to keep our distance from the organization. Even as God requires you to quit the group, God requires you to love the individuals who have entered into relationship with you. Kindness, generosity, mercy, and love must continue to flow to the person.

Quit the task that estranges you *from* God. But maintain the relationship in order to love the person *to* God.

We must accept that God has people on various timetables when it comes to His work in their lives. We must be willing to be patient in our love.

We must accept that God has people on various timetables when it comes to His work in their lives.

The Position, Power, and Perseverance of Love

At the end of his life, Dad was in a hospital. One of the things I learned is that *patients* are often required to display *patience*. Patients have to wait. Complaining gets them nowhere. It was in the hospital by my father's bedside that I learned important lessons about the position, power, and perseverance of love.

The Position of Love—Waiting

Waiting is a position. It is a state of being until what we want appears or comes to pass.

None of us likes waiting for the things we want. Think back to your childhood and the way you felt just before your birthday or Christmas. You were eager for the presents you were sure were coming—or for the festivities that you were sure were being planned. You had little concern for emotional growth or cultural significance; you only cared about the *gratification of fun!* Adults aren't much different than children. We want what we want, when we want it. Instead of saving for the material possessions we want, we whip out a credit card and hope we have enough money to pay the bill when it arrives.

My father taught me the value of waiting by not immediately giving me what I wanted. First he would make me state my case for the *need* of having a particular item, and then he would make me wait as one of the criteria for ensuring that I *really* needed, valued, or desired the item.

God often calls on us to wait for what we desire from Him— even if our desire is good and is according to His promises and will. I readily admit that I sometimes find it very difficult to stay in the position of *waiting* when I am certain that the thing I desire is in the heart of God's will.

**God often calls on us to wait for what
we desire from Him—even if our desire
is good and is according to His promises and will.**

Why does God ask us to wait? I believe part of the reason is that He doesn't want us wasting our energy seeking the things we desire. He wants us to "seek first His kingdom and His righteousness" (Matthew 6:33 NASB) and to trust Him to provide for us all the

things we need without our begging for them or using our time and
energy to find a way to make things happen in our favor!

I learned a very important lesson when I learned that God
wants me to *ask Him first* for what He wants to give me. I learned
to ask Him to show me His path for me to walk, and once I
discerned that, to show me what He would provide for me so I
might walk that path effectively and efficiently.

When my father told me to "go ask God" for what I needed,
I was just mad enough at Dad to do what he said! I went to God.
I prayed out of spite at first, but then I began to think about how
much God loved me, how He had created me and sent His Son to
die for my sins, and about how much He desired for me to trust
Him and follow Him. I asked God to show me how He wanted
Juanita and me to live. I knew with certainty that He wanted us to
pay our bills—but what I had never before asked God was, "Which
bills do you want me to have?" I asked God to help Juanita and me
get current in our finances. And God did that! Things were a bit
stressful for a while, but we always had a roof over our heads and
food on our table, and we both had jobs.

Even after our immediate financial situation was resolved,
I continued to ask God for His direction in how to plan my
financial life—and as part of that process, how to plan my work
and my obligations and my schedule and all other aspects of my
use of time and resources. How could I become more efficient
in my use of time? How could I become more productive? How
could I stop wasting time and devote those minutes and hours
to doing precisely what God wanted me to do? How could I stop

being anxious and use that energy to focus on God-given opportunities immediately at hand?

I began to look around at people I perceived as patient and started emulating them. I asked, "Why doesn't Judy freak out when the waiter doesn't immediately refill her drink?" or, "How can Bill sit there without checking his phone every ten seconds?" The more I studied people around me the more I realized that impatience rarely solves anything—it only causes frustration to brew and anger to erupt. Being restless doesn't get us what we want any sooner. It only increases our stress and agitation. Perhaps most importantly, I learned that patience can be *learned*. It can become the norm of our position in life. The Bible promises that those who *wait* on the Lord will be renewed and made strong (Isaiah 40:31).

Patience can be *learned*.
It can become the norm of our position in life.

The Power of Love—Humility

If patience is the *position* that love is to take, then humility is the *power* that a person is to display emotionally.

We err when we think that a short-fused, angry person has more emotional power than a humble, steadfast, quiet-in-spirit person. The humble person is not "stuffing" his emotions, but rather is genuinely expecting God to do *all* the heavy lifting related to moving heaven and earth to get things done.

A humble person is in the right position to see miracles and reap exceptional rewards. Humility is *power under control,* and more specifically, power under God's control.

I will never tell you that it is easy to keep your emotions in check and to stay humble before God and other people. Humility is not easy, even for the most laid-back personality. It is hard to stay even-tempered and to maintain a position of trusting God to act in *His* best timing according to *His* best methods.

What does humility look like in daily life? The foremost characteristic of everyday humility is that truly humble people refuse to transmit their pain to others. They do not give in to the urge to blast others with anger—or with righteous indignation or moral outrage. Humble people do not display a self-focused desire for power or control in order to get what they want, even if they know that what they want is perhaps best for all concerned.

Humility—genuine humility—flies in the face of our culture. We live in a world that seems to belong to bombastic, hard-hitting, competitive, and assertive people, regardless of gender, age, race, or religion. We think leaders must have a hit-you-over-the-head style to display true power and authority. This simply isn't the way Jesus led. And it isn't the way God calls His people to bring about justice and equity.

I am in full agreement with what Richard Rohr has written in *Hope against Darkness*: "'Resurrected' people prayerfully bear witness against injustice and evil—but also agree compassionately to hold their own complicity in that same evil. It is not over there, it is here. It is our problem, not *theirs*. The Risen Christ, not accidentally, still carries the wounds in his hands and side."[1]

There is no lasting value in displaying our wounds so that we bleed all over other people. There is lasting value in humbly acknowledging that we are wounded, trusting God to bind up our wounds and make us whole, and encouraging others to do the same.

There is lasting value in humbly acknowledging that we are wounded, trusting God to bind up our wounds and make us whole, and encouraging others to do the same.

The Perseverance of Love—Endurance

If patience is our position and humility is our power, then we must also come to the place where "enduring to the end" is our definition of *perseverance*.

Even though my father was not an easy man to live with—something I witnessed and Dad openly acknowledged—my mother never gave up on him or walked away from their marriage. She loved him with an active, persevering love.

As my father faced his final days, we had a talk one evening in his hospital room. He told me that he had apologized to Mom for all the moments he was less than the man she needed him to be. He told me how much he loved her for never giving up on him and how he wished he had taken a different path earlier in life.

Dad had regrets. Mom, on the other hand, had no regrets. The truth is, persevering love produces no regrets, because it is always the right choice.

**Persevering love produces no regrets,
because it is always the right choice.**

Perseverance does not call us to do more than we can do; rather, it calls us to do what we are capable of doing—nothing more, but nothing less. Perseverance calls us to live every day fully with purpose and to love to the best of our ability, as patiently and humbly as possible.

Can we always succeed every day when it comes to patience and humility? Probably not. But can we always get up the next day and *choose* with our will to persevere in loving? Yes . . . yes, indeed.

At the heart of perseverance is *forgiveness.*

Forgiveness and Perseverance Go Together

I encourage you to take a few moments and count the sins against others you have committed today in your thoughts, words, and deeds. I'm not trying to make you feel guilty—just trying to make a point! Think of the things you have done that are contrary to what you *know* are God's purposes for your life.

Now think about how many times God has forgiven you—just today. If you have sinned against Him eight or ten times . . . or ten times ten . . . how many times has God beaten you with His sovereign wooden stick in order to force you back into submission and compliance? Your guilt may make you feel as if you have been beaten, but in truth, God's words to you are loving words of forgiveness and restoration. God's promise to you is that if you admit your sins to Him, He will always forgive you, cleanse you, and put you back on the right path (1 John 1:9).

God's promise to you is that if you admit your sins to Him, He will always forgive you, cleanse you, and put you back on the right path.

If God forgives and restores us, then it is not illogical for us to reason that God desires for us to extend His example of forgiveness to others. In today's terminology, we are to "pay it forward." We are to forgive those who hurt us or reject us. We are to refuse to hold their failures and mistakes against them. We are to release them from the prison cell of our own heart and put them in the hands of our loving God.

I certainly am not saying that we are to disregard the differences between good and bad behavior, or right and wrong attitudes and beliefs. We are to *know* what God expects of us and to do it. We are to be able to discern evil from righteousness. But while we are to judge behavior, we are not to judge *people*.

To judge is to pass sentence on a person. It is to take on the role of issuing a sentence. Judging people is God's role. Our role is to point a person toward God and to *love*. There is little to be gained by holding onto resentments and bitterness, or in yelling and screaming in anger at those who have harmed us. Release the offender to God's decisions. And then continue to tell the person about Jesus' love with a tempered attitude.

Keep on Keeping On

Patience, humility, and perseverance are what give us a no-quit ability to love.

If you are struggling to "keep on keeping on" with someone you *know* God has put you into relationship to love, ask yourself:

- Is God finished loving me? If not, how can I say I am finished loving this person?
- Is God railing at me, exerting His vast power to force me to conform to His desires? If not, how can I rise up and demand that this person live the way I dictate or demand?
- Is God throwing in the towel and abandoning me to my own lousy choices and bad decisions? If not, how can I fail to persevere in being the best witness I can be to the love and enduring presence of Jesus?

Love doesn't quit. Period.

Responding . . .

1. Who do you count on *always* being in your corner, *always* having your back? On what basis do you have the assurance this person or people will *always* be there for you?

2. Have you ever experienced God leading you to quit a particular task or affiliation? How did you feel about that? What did you do? If God led you to end the job or affiliation, how did you feel after you made that decision and parted ways?

3. "We are to love the people, but we may need to keep our distance from the organization." How do you respond to this statement? What are the difficulties in separating yourself from a bad situation or an ungodly alliance, and still loving an individual who is in the group or company you are leaving?

4. What struggles to you have when it comes to:

    patience?

    humility?

    perseverance?

    How did you—or how are you attempting to—deal with these struggles?

CHAPTER 5

Love Must Be Learned

Every person on earth *learns* to hate or to love. We are not born with these emotions or behaviors fully formed. We are born with a propensity to rebel against authority, including the authority of God and the authority of parents and others who rule over us. But we are not born with strong emotions of hate or love that compel us to engage in words and deeds that are overtly and strongly hateful or loving.

Who taught you to hate? And what to hate?

Who taught you to love? And what to love?

There are many people who need to relearn what they have been taught. And the process of relearning love always involves the truth that God has given us a higher way in His Word.

As followers of Jesus, we can count on the Word of God telling us the truth about God's faithfulness and loving-kindness—we can trust God's Word to be true when it comes to God loving us and sending Jesus to die on our behalf so we can be forgiven and one day live forever with God in heaven. We can trust the

Word of God when it tells the truth about the evil of Satan and our need for rejecting evil and pursuing what God says is good.

The process of relearning love always involves the truth that God has given us a higher way in His Word.

We also can count on God to give us human examples to follow and to help us know how to apply His principles. These human examples teach us how to love in practical ways.

We can learn from good examples and from bad examples. The good teachers about love give us information that we can apply, verify, and find joy in living out. We learn from them what to do, say, and believe. The bad teachers give us information that we are wise to reject—we can learn from them what *not* to do, say, or believe.

One factor related to the way we learn love, or hate, is often overlooked. We learn our basic attitude toward life and other people from someone who has a leadership role in our life. The leader may not be of our choosing—such as a parent, teacher, or perhaps a Sunday school teacher, pastor, or coach who is a leader for us in our childhood. The leader may be a good leader or a bad leader. Either way, we are in a follower position and someone else is in a position of authority. The leaders in our lives exert authority over us, and whether they like it and embrace it or not, they also have a degree of *responsibility* that goes along with their authority. Leadership is a powerful sword with two sides: authority (power) and responsibility (serving).

Although my primary experience with leadership as a child came from my parents and they are my prime examples in this chapter, I am aware that *any* person who is in *any* leadership position is challenged to recognize that he or she is a teacher of values, and the foremost value is love. To be a good leader, any leader *must* teach those who follow him or her—all those under his or her authority and for whom he or she bears responsibility—the importance of choosing love over hate. Love is the foremost lesson a leader must teach. Not just some of the time. All of the time.

Love is the foremost lesson a leader
must teach. Not just some of the time.
All of the time.

Love Lessons from My Mom

I was extremely fortunate in my life to have a mother who loved me dearly and never quit on me. She chose to *love. Period.* She modeled unconditional, persistent, steadfast love for me. She taught me the importance of love.

I was precocious as a child, and I suffered from what is now called attention deficit disorder (ADD). I was also highly mischievous.

My mother didn't care how bright and talented I was, how much ADD I had, or how clever I was in my mischief. My mother specialized in right and wrong, and she had a clear understanding about what was acceptable behavior for my safety and for my growth and development. She also had a strong opinion that adults are in charge and children aren't. My mother set very clear parameters for what she would tolerate and wouldn't tolerate.

I knew the boundaries, which meant I knew when I was stepping outside them. I knew with certainty that when I stepped beyond Mom's parameters and was caught doing so, I could count on Mom to unleash her "weapon of mass destruction": her big, powerful, country-girl left hand. The tears that accompanied her discourse went something like this: "After all I do for you, you go and do something like this? I am going to whip your behind because if I don't, somebody else will when you grow up and leave this house. I love you . . ." and then the spanking would come. I never doubted that my mom loved me because she was willing to discipline me when I stepped outside of her clearly defined and consistent parameters.

Parenting is a leadership responsibility that encompasses every aspect of guidance, regardless of activity. My mom, like all parents and all leaders, was less than perfect because she is a human being, and all human beings are prone to mistakes, misjudgments, and missteps in life. We must never expect our leaders to be perfect—either perfect in their own character or perfect in the way they exert leadership over us. At the same time, we are wise to choose the best leaders—not because of what they might do for us, but because of what they might model for us and require of us when it comes to love and hate.

Three Qualities of Loving Leadership

Even in the midst of our error-prone human frailty, we can look for four main qualities that can help us learn how to love— *period*—when it comes to parenthood, as well as any other type of authority.

Consistency

My mom was a model of consistency. She lived a disciplined, orderly life and she desired the same for me. She modeled for me the truth that it is far easier to keep the rules and reap the rewards for obedience than to rebel and experience the consequences of rebellion.

If Mom and Dad argued, I could count on a consistency at the end of their arguments. They would remind me that their challenges and differences of opinion had nothing to do with the fact that they both loved me. They called their tensions "grown folks' business"—and as a result, I grew up knowing that I preferred *not* to have much "grown folks' business" in my relationships. From my early childhood, I preferred to agree rather than disagree.

I knew that the boundary lines for behavior were not going to shift from day to day. If Mom and Dad believed something was wrong today, I could count on it being wrong tomorrow. I might tiptoe along some of those boundaries and occasionally cross a line, but I also knew that my punishment would be just, swift, and painful. In my home, there was consistency in the consequences as well as in the rules.

I could also count on the fact that Mom and Dad couldn't be played against each other. If Mom had set a rule, Dad required me to abide by it, and vice versa.

Integrity

My mom never lied to me. She created an environment of truth and integrity within our home. Mom believed what she said and said what she believed. She required the same from me.

She conveyed the message, "This is the one place where you must always tell the truth because the people in this house have your back." Because my parents never lied to me, I saw every aspect of both of my parents' lives—the beautiful and the not-so-beautiful. They were very transparent to me. They didn't put up a false front or try to convince me they were something they weren't.

I discovered later in life that most children don't grow up seeing much of the negative in their parents' lives. Their parents become their superheroes, and when the scales of that fantasy fall from their eyes somewhere around adolescence, they discover that Mom and Dad aren't infallible, and the disappointment can be great. The scales were removed from my eyes early in life, and the result was a healthy family environment.

I learned to live authentically because my parents required truth telling and transparent living from me. If I displayed any negative traits . . . well, that was an opportunity to learn the truth about admitting fault, making amends, and offering and receiving apologies and forgiveness.

Dignity

Dignity conveys worth. Dignity says, "I respect you because I see you as being worthy of my time and energy. I believe in you enough to want to commit my time to your improvement and betterment."

When we extend dignity to another human being, we ourselves are simultaneously embodied with dignity. A dignified person has a bearing of confidence and strength that sends a message to the world: "I am worthy. I am a human being loved by God and therefore, I am worthy of respect. I am someone who can and will be a force for good in your life—I have the capability of being a good friend, a good employee, a good spouse, a good parent, a good role model, a good supervisor, a good neighbor, and a good advocate."

My mother taught me by her example and her words that God is good all the time, and all the time God is good. She also taught me that God desires to help us to become more and more like Him. He counted us worthy to send His Son to die on our behalf so He might live with us forever. God gives us dignity, if we will only receive it and walk in it.

Love Lessons from My Dad

Even though my dad was not a model Christian during my growing-up years, he was a leader who taught me tremendous lessons about how to live a life that was truthful and marked by dignity.

My father never lied to me, regardless of the consequences. He kept his word, regardless of the personal cost to him. He was a keen observer of circumstances, and he insisted that I know the situations I faced and was prepared to act in a way that kept me from being conned or tricked.

My father was an independent thinker, but he was willing to learn from others and he believed in the collaborative process. He believed that most people were incapable of showing compassion for longer than a couple of weeks—after that time period, they tended to return to their daily routines and forget those who needed help or caregiving.

Dad was quick to tell others that he appreciated them. He regularly asked church folks to pray for him, and he honored friendship. If he made a mistake, he apologized quickly. And he made some necessary corrections for mistakes he made early in his life.

My father laughed a lot every day, knew how to keep a secret, and negotiated regularly. He worked relentlessly and rarely took breaks. He drove his cars until they had no remaining value, and then he would get angry if he failed to sell a car for more than it was worth. He made sure Mom had the best he could provide. He never met a stranger, and He could curse better than most people can quote poetry.

My father even allowed himself to learn from *me*. A few years after I had quit the motel business and Dad had told me to "go ask God," he started to pay attention to how I was living my life. He saw that I practiced what I preached and that I accepted others no matter their situation. He saw that I refused to believe the gospel is only for a certain group of people—rather, it makes room for everyone Jesus accepts. And Jesus never marginalized, excluded, or threw away any person.

It was a surprise to me, but a joy, when Dad began to attend St. John's, the church I now serve as pastor.

One day Dad's friends asked him, "Why now, at age seventy, have you finally come to God?" Dad responded, "Because I finally met a preacher I trust!"

My father continued to attend church and learned more about faith and about God's love and forgiveness. He came to accept that God loves unconditionally and that God treats people with respect and acceptance, regardless of the way they dress or act or where they come from.

When the doctors told my father he had only a few weeks left to live, he responded, "Well, I will live every day like I will live forever." And he did.

My father died on July 4, 2004. I lost my dad *and* my best friend. I cried because God had allowed us to work our way through the tough times. We had been able to forgive each other and tell each other how much we loved each other. I cried because my dad was my teacher when it came to the power of love over hate.

My father taught me also that good leaders have the ability to be led. Good leaders are always looking for a better way to live, and for a higher standard of behavior.

Perhaps more than any other person, Dad taught me the unwavering significance of unconditional love. And I am grateful that I could be instrumental in his life in conveying God's love back to him. Dad was my teacher and my lesson, and he was also my reward.

**Perhaps more than any other person,
Dad taught me the unwavering significance
of unconditional love.**

Without doubt, love in our hearts that leads to love in our actions is the key to the growth of faith.

Responding . . .

1. Whom are you teaching today? Over whom do you have influence? Over whom do you have authority, and for whom do you have responsibility?

2. What are you teaching others about love?

3. What are the major lessons about love that you learned from your parents? Do you have an active outlet for passing on these lessons to the next generation?

CHAPTER 6

Love Is Kind

My wife, Juanita, and I met at a funeral. We often say it was one of the best funerals we ever attended!

I recall looking over my shoulder at this funeral—one of my infrequent visits to a church at that time—and being distracted by a glowing young woman with incredible legs. I looked over my shoulder as much as I could during that event, wondering who she was and how I might meet her.

At the end of the funeral I made my way to my mother to ask if she knew this young woman. She said, "Yes, that's Silver's niece."

I said, "Can you introduce me to Silver?" She said, "Sure," and off we went to meet Aunt Silver. We exchanged pleasantries and Aunt Silver introduced me to Juanita's mother, who in turned called over Juanita to introduce me to her. I was working that room like a man on fire!

There was something about Juanita that told me from my first glance she was unique, but I couldn't define it at that moment. We chatted briefly and then prepared to get in our cars and move to the burial place. I hopped out of my car with the intent of lining up a date with her, but she had a plan to line up an *appointment* with me. Juanita sold insurance, and she was good at it! We ultimately had our date/appointment and I bought the insurance policy hook, line, and sinker. We continued to see each other regularly for several months until "The Voice" paid me an unexpected visit.

"The Voice" was what I called my conscience—the inner compass that had guided me up to that point through danger, relationships, and various business dealings. Every once in a while, my inward prompting would tell me, *Exit now* or, *Don't trust this person.* Occasionally The Voice—which I now understand to be the Holy Spirit—would make a strange request.

When I met Juanita, in a moment of earth-pounding clarity, The Voice said to me, *Never do anything that would cause this woman to stop trusting you.*

At that point in my life I was completely untrustworthy, so this request hit me like a ton of bricks. Juanita was the kindest, purest, most honest person I had ever met. The only way I could honor The Voice at that moment was to stop interacting with Juanita. So, after dinner later that week, we parted without my telling her what The Voice had said to me. The next day, neither she nor I made our customary call to check in from the night before. A week went by, then a month, and before I knew it, a year had passed. Our lives had moved apart without any further communication, and we never had a discussion about why we had suddenly stopped seeing each other.

During that year I often wondered how Juanita was doing, and she sometimes bumped into people who asked her, "Do you know a guy named Rudy Rasmus?" I searched my soul for the reason behind this unusual request from The Voice. And at the end of the year, The Voice returned with a new request for me to call Juanita. I did immediately, without hesitation. She answered the phone and I asked how she was doing. She said, "Great." I asked if she was available for lunch. She said yes. We were married six months later.

I had no idea what God was up to. Years before this, I had moved away from God. I had grown up going to a church where I attended service to catch up on my naps. I stopped attending church after I moved to Dallas with my parents. In college, I became a marginal Buddhist. I was intrigued by the idea of peaceful enlightenment and meditation. After college I explored Islam and stayed on that path until I decided to leave the road of religion entirely. I had pursued nothing but an extended preoccupation with contempt, cynicism, and critique for all things related to spiritual life. It had been a long, dark road for years, but God never left me alone.

**It had been a long, dark road for years,
but God never left me alone.**

God in Steady Pursuit

God sent three people after me. The first two were childhood friends who reconnected with me after I returned to Houston to join my dad in business. The first person was a guy named Ivory Smith.

Ivory would stop by the motel we owned with cassette tapes of sermons, books, and other ministry items, mostly tracts, that were designed to scare the hell out of people on the wrong path. Those things were effective, because I could always see myself as being the person who needed that message! I felt God definitely knew far more about me than I was comfortable with Him knowing. For years, Ivory would stop by with regularity and would remind me that God loved me. He never pushed or insisted that I comply with anything. He just shared how good God is.

The second person God sent after me was my elementary-school buddy Howard Watson. Howard had been a committed follower of Jesus from a very early age. His church was in our old neighborhood, and Howard often invited me to the Sunday evening worship service. Occasionally I would accept his invitation and always felt love from the people at Shady Acres Church of Christ. The people there were warm and devoted.

Howard became a minister in that church while we were still young men, and I always respected his commitment to what he believed to be true about God. I even felt a slight tug at times during the services, but I quickly turned and ran in the other direction, remembering that my father said, "Religion is bad for business"— which was true, given the business we were in during those days.

I managed to escape the attempts of both Ivory and Howard to get me "saved." The third person was not so easily avoided. Her name was Juanita.

After we married, it became clear that Juanita and I were headed to church with great regularity on Sundays, regardless of what I thought about the idea. The problem for her was finding a church that I would attend without a barrage of contempt, cynicism, and critique after each service. Juanita, however, was not only a committed follower of Jesus, but she was feisty!

We finally found a church I liked—Windsor Village United Methodist—and a pastor I could trust, Kirbyjon Caldwell. There we encountered a community of people who were not afraid to *love—period.*

More Than Random Acts of Kindness

My journey of love had really begun the moment I met Juanita. I had instantly trusted her. And as an extension of that trust, I trusted her faith in God. Juanita had an unconditional love that manifested itself in profound examples of kindness—perhaps the greatest ongoing acts of kindness I had ever known. Juanita did not engage in various random acts of kindness; rather, kindness flowed from her like a continuous stream, permeating everything she said and did.

In 1990, after we had been married five years, I joined her as a Christian. Two years later, we entered ministry, thanks to our friend, pastor, and mentor Kirbyjon Caldwell. And St. John's Church—where I now pastor—was also "born again" after its initial start as a faith community.

When I say that Juanita has loved and extended kindness continually, I do not mean to imply that her life has been easy or that kindness is always easy for her to display. Far from it.

In 1992, we started St. John's.

In 1999, seven years later, Juanita suffered a major episode with depression that was rooted in an undiagnosed physical condition.

In 2000, she was diagnosed with tuberculosis.

In 2001, while doctors were checking her lungs, one of her lungs was punctured.

In 2010, she was diagnosed with kidney cancer.

Any one of those events would be enough to cause many people to clock out—on faith, on the Lord, on kindness. Juanita's faith, however, was stronger than depression, extreme pain, and a catastrophic medical diagnosis. Her faith and her love gave her the tremendous capability to show kindness in the face of extreme negativity. Let me assure you, I know from personal experience that two people really can become one when kindness is the bonding agent holding them together.

Two people really can become one when kindness is the bonding agent holding them together.

Kindness during Cancer

When Juanita was diagnosed with cancer in 2010, my world was rocked beyond imagination. My faith was rocked as well. I could not believe that I was hearing the words "You have cancer" come out of the doctor's mouth as he spoke with Juanita. It seemed to me as if a movie we were in had suddenly shifted into slow motion and that all of the air was sucked out of the room, leaving us gasping.

I need to be a little more honest—Juanita seemed just fine in that moment. I was the one who was gasping emotionally for my next breath. I felt abandoned by God.

Juanita did not waver in her trust in God's goodness. She faced the moment with a degree of courage I have seldom witnessed. From somewhere deep within her faith, she heard God speaking to her that she would be healed. I, on the other hand, heard nothing.

When we searched the Internet to learn more about the type of cancer she had, the name of the number one surgeon in the world who dealt with that type of cancer popped up. And when Juanita was admitted to MD Anderson, one of the top-rated cancer hospitals in the world, guess who became her doctor? The surgeon recommended immediate surgery, but to my shock, Juanita said no. Juanita told me that she had heard from God that surgery would not be needed at that time. But I had heard nothing to that effect from God.

Later that day, I said one of the dumbest things I have ever said in my life. I told Juanita, "If you die while waiting on God to give you the go-ahead, then I am through with God."

Our home became incredibly silent for the next month as Juanita moved through her process with God and I also moved through a process with God. Juanita would give me "the look," turn her attention to God, and somehow extend kindness to me while I was flailing around in doubt and despair. For three months, her *kindness as a conversation with God* communicated with me the reality that kindness is not only something God shows us on a regular basis, but kindness is also something we are to show God on a regular basis!

**Kindness is not only something God shows us
on a regular basis, but kindness is also something
we are to show God on a regular basis!**

The *reciprocity of kindness* is what makes kindness visible to the world around us. Juanita understood this from a deep, contemplative place refined by hours of prayer and communication with God. Three months after her first meeting with the surgeon, Juanita agreed to surgery and the surgeon removed her right kidney. She had a malignant, eight-centimeter tumor. Juanita remained kind. Later she said that her kidney was the price of tuition for the class she took on the need to be kind to herself.

Steps to Loving Yourself

In the months and years since her cancer surgery, Juanita has said that she didn't find her voice to speak to women until she had lived through the crises she experienced. Her message has taken the form of "Steps to Loving Yourself." She regularly speaks on this theme now, and below is just a portion of the wisdom she conveys, mostly to women and especially to mothers and daughters.

Lesson #1: Be Kind to Yourself

Love yourself. Become a friend to yourself. It is not up to any other person to encourage you or speak kindness to you. It is up to *you* to speak kindness to yourself.

Lesson #2: Acknowledge Your Emotions

Every person feels fear, pain, resentment, guilt, loneliness, grief, sorrow, depression, and other negative emotions from time to time. Don't stifle the inner screams of these emotions. Face your negative emotions and give voice to them. Don't judge yourself for feeling negative. Rather, acknowledge that you *do* feel negative and then consciously and intentionally hand those negative feelings over to God so He can heal them.

You may need to pause your life for a while to isolate your true feelings. Take the time you need to do that. The pause can make all the difference in your ability to identify your deepest fears.

Lesson #3: Affirm What God Says about You

Go to God's Word. Spend time talking with God. Listen closely to what God says about who you are to Him and what He desires for you. God considers you to be His beloved child, and He desires the best for you. Let that truth sink deep within you.

Speak aloud to yourself what God says. Create a CD or MP3 that you can play back to yourself. Write God's words to you in dry-erase marker on your bathroom mirror and say them out loud often. Make up a new song, or two or three or four, to express what God says.

Don't question whether this is a good thing to do. Just do it! God's Word tells us that as a person thinks in her heart, so she *is* (Proverbs 23:7). Faith comes by *hearing* the truth of God's Word (Romans 10:17).

If you say something that is not according to God's Word, push the Delete button. Listen closely to your own speech. If you find yourself saying something such as, "I'm sick and tired of . . . ," recognize that you've just sent a message to your own brain that you are sick and tired! Speak a new language that is rooted in your faith that God *is* in control of all things at all times, and God *is* working behind the scenes to conform all things to your good, now and forever.

**Speak a new language that is rooted
in your faith that God *is* in control
of all things at all times.**

Lesson #4: Apply Your Energy Daily

Do what you can do with the energy you have for each day. Don't beat yourself up because you don't have more energy or don't have all the energy you would like to have. Use what you do have. Ask God to renew you so that you are capable of fulfilling His plans and purposes for you—one step at a time, one day at a time.

What I've Learned about Kindness from Juanita

The four lessons that Juanita outlined above are ones I've seen her live out. Juanita's kindness in the face of all sorts of reasons to be unkind is testimony to me that the lessons she has learned are valuable lessons that *every* person can learn.

If you are struggling with a problem in your life, check your emotional response to that problem. Does your problem make you angry? Does it make you hateful? Does it cause you to place all sorts of conditions on others when it comes to their friendship, help, or advice? Does your problem make you feel like a victim or have expectations that other people should do more for you or treat you better? Is your problem becoming your excuse?

Most importantly, is your problem impacting what you believe about God?

Is your problem impacting
what you believe about God?

I have encountered so many people in my life who take the approach, "If God is a loving and good God, why does He allow . . ." A person can tie himself up in knots with that line of thinking. There are no good answers to questions that begin, "If God . . ."

The truth is, God exists. He has ways and purposes and plans that are far higher than anything we can comprehend. He loves us more deeply and more completely than we can ever love ourselves or be loved by any other person.

In the midst of our troubles and needs—our deepest sorrows and greatest questions—God asks only that we trust Him. There is nothing to be gained by moving away from God. Yet there is comfort and love to be gained by burrowing into God and clinging to Him with all our heart, mind, soul, and strength.

**In the midst of our troubles and needs—
our deepest sorrows and greatest questions—
God asks only that we trust Him.**

Bad situations cry out to us, "Can you trust God with *this*?" The answer is, "I don't have any recourse but to trust God with this and everything else!"

There is no other heavenly Father.

There is no other Savior.

There is no other path worth walking in this life.

There is no other source of all things necessary, no other fountain of love, no other power that heals and makes us whole.

Reject the Lies

When we consider the problems in our lives, we must refrain from adopting these opinions.

Lie #1: God Is Angry with Me

God is not angry with you; He loves you. He may be angry at the enemy of your soul, who has tricked you into believing a lie, or at the conditions that have produced a negative outcome for you. But when it comes to *you*, you are His beloved child and God is with you in the midst of your trouble to help you as no other person, institution, or force can do.

Lie #2: God Is Punishing Me

God is not punishing you with the problem in your life. God can use a negative situation to teach you important lessons for your future or to use you to teach others important lessons about God and His love—but God does not seek to destroy, maim, or impair His children! God loves you.

Rather than think that God is angry or that He is lashing out at us in punishment, we need to ask, "What can I do to alleviate this suffering? What would God have me do to show others His love and kindness through my suffering?"

"What would God have me do to show others His love and kindness through my suffering?"

Lie #3: The Devil Is Busy

If you blame all bad situations and circumstances on the devil, you likely will find yourself quickly trapped into taking no responsibility for your own mistakes or the human frailties and errors that are truly at the root of many bad, unjust, and debilitating situations in our world.

God's Word tells us that the devil is a liar, and it seems to me that one of his choicest lies is the lie that he is too powerful for us to overcome him. If the devil is able to convince us that he is too powerful for us to fight and defeat, then he will stop us from displaying the kindness that can reverse many bad situations and turn them to good.

Rather than rail against the devil, we are wise to proclaim that God can and will work in us and through us to bring about His good purposes!

Make Sense of the Pain

The way to make sense of your pain is to see it as an example of the truth that *you* are not in control of the universe. In fact, you are in control of only one thing: how you will choose to respond to God's love.

The way to make sense of your pain is to see it as an example of the truth that *you* are not in control of the universe.

Furthermore, the response you choose to make—in the midst of the terrible diagnosis or the bad prognosis, in the midst of the breakdown, shakedown, or turndown times—will dictate what you are going to do with God's love and how you are going to apply it to your life and to the lives of others around you.

It was only when I fully accepted the fact that I was not in control of Juanita's cancer diagnosis, or any other problem in her life or mine, that I was able to move into a deep inner experience in which the light of God's love became the only light necessary on the immediate path in front of me. It was the light of that intimate, quiet, glowing love of God that fueled my faith to do the next thing that was good and right to do. God's love gave me the ability to be kind and to show love—one step at a time.

Set a Goal of Kindness

I challenge you to set a goal: "Be kind to someone today."

Most people can do well with that goal. It's tougher, however, if you set this goal: "My goal is to be kind to someone I am not normally kind to."

In many cases, an act of kindness is the first step toward expressing love to someone who desperately needs love. That someone may be you. It may be a member of your family. It may be a total stranger.

**In many cases, an act of kindness is the first step
toward expressing love to someone
who desperately needs love.**

Let me make these suggestions as you establish a target for your kindness.

Leave Your Expectations at the Door

Expectations are premeditated resentments. When you begin to expect somebody to act in a certain way or respond to you in a certain way, you are prejudging them before they have a chance to do *anything*! Then, if the person lives up to your expectations of bad behavior, you feel justified in your bitterness, resentment, or anger.

Take a different approach. Choose to extend kindness without *any* expectations of the person to whom you are extending kindness.

Consider your set of expectations—those things others expect you to routinely say or do. Since I'm a pastor, I'm usually expected to be happy all the time and to give good advice. The reality is that nobody is happy 100 percent of the time, and sometimes my advice doesn't always help a person as much as I want or the person seeking advice wants. The same is likely true for your life and the expectations others have of *you*. Nobody is perfect.

Once you accept that you can't live up to everyone else's expectations of you, it will become easier for you to let go of your expectations of others.

Once you accept that you can't live up to everyone else's expectations of you, it will become easier for you to let go of your expectations of others.

Try to help others work beyond their foibles and achieve their dreams. Lend a hand. Give support. Give a word of encouragement or genuine compliment. When another person sees that you don't expect him to be a superhero, he may very well take a major step toward becoming what he *can* be.

Make a List and Check It Twice

One of the biggest reasons we aren't kind to one another seems to be this: we forget that we are *dependent* on the kindness of others. Nobody gets through a single day without someone else's help, even if it's the help of the guy who invented the alarm clock that gets you going in the morning. We cannot survive, at least mentally, if we don't have somebody supporting, encouraging, or teaching us in some way.

Make a list of the things you need help in doing—and then, next to each of these daily or long-term needs, write the name of at least one person who assists you. You may say, for example, "Well, I can dress myself with nobody else's assistance." Really? Did you make all of the clothing you wear in a given day? From fabric that you wove yourself? From elements that you grew yourself? On land that you tilled yourself and acquired totally on your own? Did you wash or dry-clean all of your own garments? Did you have anybody's help in choosing the garments most flattering to your body? Did you rely on anybody to tell you if something is wrong with your clothing before you put your worst foot forward outside the door of your house?

No, you very likely are not *totally* responsible for dressing yourself.

The more you acknowledge that you need help from others to do even the most basic chores, accomplish the simplest tasks, and maintain a modicum of good humor and intelligence, the more you are in a better position to treat others with the kindness that says, "You are a worthy person on this earth who contributes to the whole of the world we share."

Never allow yourself to become too proud to help another person or too proud to receive the help of another.

I certainly encourage you to do all you can to provide for your own daily and long-term needs, but I also encourage you to think of your community, your nation, and the world. What might you do to make life better for others who live across town or in poverty both close by and abroad? What might you do to bring joy into the life of those who don't experience joy and to bring a bit of laughter into the lives of those who seem swallowed up by sadness?

Never allow yourself to become too proud to help another person or too proud to receive the help of another.

Focus on the Positives

Most of us in our American society have been trained to work hard for the things we have. We go to our jobs with an assumption that, if we do our best, we will be rewarded. Yet the best rewards we can give ourselves include a sense of *gratitude* for what we have and a sense of *appreciation* for those who treat us with respect.

If someone is holding open a door for you or picking up your trash, make sure to let that person know you appreciate his or her actions. Sometimes all it takes to motivate and encourage another human being is to say simply, "Hey, you're doing a good job," or to offer a sincere thank-you.

I have found that if I can offer a positive word to someone, I usually get much better service and experience far fewer problems. The next time you go to a restaurant, look around for the good things that are happening there. Thank the waitstaff for the service they are giving you. Let people know what you appreciate about your dining experience. Give compliments where compliments are deserved, and be genuine as you give voice to what you like about someone or about what the person has produced or given in service.

Positivity breeds positivity. And the more earnest we are with our appreciation, the more our kindness is returned to us. I'm not saying that you should use kindness in a manipulative way in order to receive kindness; rather, it is a basic fact of human nature that if we express kindness, we are likely to receive kindness in return. Somebody has to start that love ball bouncing around a room or office or church . . . it might as well be you!

If we express kindness, we are likely to receive kindness in return.

Whose Kindness Is It?

In the end, we need to remember that any act of kindness we show to others is an extension of the kindness that God has shown to us through Christ Jesus. He is the One who reached out to us first. He is the One who sends us countless messages in any given day that say, *I love you. I made this sunrise for you to enjoy. I caused these flowers to bloom to give you pleasure. I kept you safe when that driver swerved into your lane. I gave you the ideas that moved your project at work forward. I helped you comfort a grieving coworker. I gave you eyes to see the world the way I see it and a heart to respond to the world the way I feel about it.*

The kindness of God is *always* worthy of being extended to others. Even the smallest of kind gestures, given with sincerity, can be used to soften a person's heart and turn the person toward God.

The kindness of God is *always* worthy of being extended to others.

Love is kind. Always.

Responding . . .

1. In what ways do you recognize kindness when you encounter it?
2. Can you recall a time in which a small act of kindness made a big difference in your own life or in the life of someone you know?
3. In your opinion, why do some people find it difficult to be kind? Why—and when—do *you* find kindness difficult?

CHAPTER 7

Love Honors Others

During the spring of 2012, I witnessed one of the most impassioned fights I'd ever seen in Houston. Some readers may think that because of my past, I am referring to a fight between two people with sinister backgrounds, duking it out in the back alleys of an inner-city ghetto. This fight, however, wasn't at all like that. It was between people we would consider part of civilized society. It took place in Houston's city hall, and it pitted some members of the city council against various groups in the community.

The issue that spawned the fight involved feeding Houston's homeless people in area parks and on the city's street corners. Nobody was concerned that charitable organizations were giving away food to the homeless. This was not considered a bad thing. What brought about the fight was that there was often a lot of trash remaining in the areas after the food was served.

Complaints were lodged about the Styrofoam cups and trays tossed helter-skelter in public parks. Concern was voiced that these items often had food remaining on them, and this food attracted various creatures that represented a threat to the public health of those who visited and used the parks.

A related issue involved what was perceived to be a waste of food in some locations, with excess food being thrown away rather than being stored or frozen to distribute to other needy people elsewhere in the city.

Finally, there was the issue that there were no regulations related to the quality of the food being served. Nobody thought the charitable organizations were trying to poison the homeless. Far from it! The worry was that food may have been exposed to Houston's hot, humid weather for too long before it was consumed and that this tainted food might cause sickness.

An ordinance was suggested to the city council, and a vote was scheduled. Before the vote could be cast, however, the opponents of the ordinance wanted to voice their opinions. Opponents felt the ordinance was tantamount to the city of Houston putting up a sign on its city limits that said, "Please do not feed the homeless." Issues related to freedom of choice and freedom of religion were hauled out for examination.

At the beginning of this fight, it made sense to me to side with the opponents of the ordinance. I was, and still am, the leader of a church that has a significant homeless constituency. St. John's has a large food distribution organization we call a Food Fair. This organization is connected to our ministry partner, The Bread of Life. Over the years, I've had the privilege of personally knowing and respecting thousands of homeless men, women, and children. We have served millions of hot meals and provided support services to people on the brink of disaster, and at least three thousand homeless or transitioning individuals have joined our faith community as members.

I also know several individuals who work outside of St. John's with a similar purpose. Two of my friends have served meals to the needy in the Houston area for many years. The numbers they serve are huge. One of the agencies works with forty-eight churches in Houston, serving seventy-five hundred meals a week. If the ordinance passed, then these conscientious, caring providers would have been negatively impacted. What could I do other than disagree with an ordinance that would limit the ability of these generous, kindhearted people to serve homeless people with genuine needs?

In spite of all my connections to the opponents' side, however, I still had to listen to the arguments of the ordinance's supporters—and frankly, what they said made a lot of sense. When the ban on serving charitable meals was passed on April 4, 2012, by a vote of eleven to six, I found myself agreeing with the vote. Even though there are many great groups in Houston and throughout the United States and the rest of the world who do the Lord's work day after day as they serve the homeless and put together nutritious meals to help them, we also must remember that we live in a society of *neighbors*. We must do our service to others in ways that are responsible, respectful, and healthful.

We live in a society of *neighbors*.
We must do our service to others in ways that are
responsible, respectful, and healthful.

Love Lessons from
an Impromptu Picnic

A Christian can hardly address the issue of feeding the homeless without referencing the story of Jesus feeding multitudes of His followers on a hillside in Galilee. It is one of the first stories most children learn in Sunday school. Often a loaf of bread is used as a prop, and I feel certain that more than one child has had high expectations that the loaf of bread held in the teacher's hands will be multiplied in a mysterious way to serve everybody present at the church that day!

The Bible story reads like a happy, impromptu picnic. But the message runs much deeper than a simple provision of food.

There are actually two instances in the New Testament in which Jesus fed thousands of people. The story as it is told in the gospel of Mark pictures Jesus in the midst of a mass of people who have come to hear Him teach and see Him heal the sick and cast out demons. About four thousand families had come to the outdoor meeting, and they no doubt were very hungry and thirsty by the time the third day of meetings rolled around. Jesus called His disciples aside and said, "This crowd is breaking my heart. They have stuck with me for three days, and now they have nothing to eat. If I send them home hungry, they'll faint along the way—some of them have come a long distance" (Mark 8:2–3).

Jesus wanted to honor those who had been willing to sacrifice their time for Him. He wanted to help the people who had gathered to listen to His teaching. He desired to make sure these people had sufficient food to give them the strength and energy to get home safely. For three days Jesus had given them spiritual food. Now was the time to give them something very practical to meet their physical need.

There was just one problem: there wasn't any food. Or at least not enough to feed so many people. The large crowd had gathered far from the nearest town, which didn't have sufficient bread and fish for a crowd that size, even if they had sent enough carts and people with enough money to buy all the food in the town.

When the disciples of Jesus pointed out to Him that they were in the middle of nowhere, Jesus asked how much bread they had. They told Him that the only food in the entire crowd was a few loaves of bread and a few small fish. That was enough for Jesus. He asked the disciples to cluster the people in sections to sit on the grass, and then Jesus blessed the food that was available and began to hand it to the disciples to pass out to the people. The Bible tells us, "The people ate and were satisfied. Afterward the disciples picked up seven basketfuls of broken pieces that were left over" (Mark 8:8 NIV).

That day, Jesus honored those who had come to hear Him teach, preach, and heal—and He did it in a gracious, generous, very practical way.

When you honor someone, you put your pride on the side and let it wait there while you help another person with his or her problems.

**When you honor someone, you put your pride
on the side and let it wait there while you
help another person with his or her problems.**

Honor is looking at another person and saying, "We may not be the same, and we may not have the same ideals, but you are a human being and I am a human being and we are in this boat together. So I am going to help you."

The challenge is deepened when we recognize that we have a responsibility to honor *all* the people involved in any particular situation. It is very difficult not to choose sides!

In the case of most efforts to help the homeless, showing honor to the homeless people tends to get lost when people start to address the practical issues of *how* to help them. Individual personalities and personal goals often get in the way when various methods are proposed for helping.

Are We Helping or Hurting?

Since 1992, the people of St. John's have served a hot meal every day to those who come to us. We estimate that we have served more than a million meals to hungry people, and we have distributed at least five thousand tons of fresh food to hungry Houston families during the past twenty years.

I felt perfectly fine about the good work we were doing until I took a trip to India. That trip forced me to ask, "What do people really *need*? Are we helping or hurting them?" I asked the questions while I was in India. I had to face answers back in Houston!

For years I had felt that I *knew* what the homeless community needed, and I did my best to move our organization lockstep toward meeting those needs. Suddenly I had to ask myself, "Are these the actual needs the homeless community feels, or are these needs I have internalized as priorities?"

Don't get me wrong. As a result of our community pulling together we have done some amazing things to help one of Houston's most marginalized communities, and we have been able to extend this work far beyond the city limits of Houston.

I am grateful for the assistance offered to us by the extraordinary entertainer Beyoncé Knowles. She opened her huge pop music platform to me, and I was able to travel with her during concert tours to discuss food insufficiency in partnership with domestic and global agencies such as Feeding America and the Global FoodBanking Network. Through her generosity, I was able to speak to thousands of concertgoers from the stage during her concerts on the plight of hunger in America and in the world. Beyoncé's mother, Tina Knowles, has extended her influence in supporting the Miss a Meal initiative, which is designed to bring even more awareness to the plight of the poor and hungry in America, as well as awareness of hunger and poverty in Africa. We have raised at least $100 million so far to address the challenges of poverty around the world.

In spite of these great works and phenomenal ideas, I still ask, "What do people really *need*?" The only way we can get to the heart of the answer is to ask the people we perceive as needing help. When I started asking, I was amazed at some of the answers the needy gave me.

I still ask, "What do people really *need*?"

The problem with domestic charity is that solutions are often wrapped up in a complex package of poverty, mental illness, incarceration, substance abuse, educational system failures, do-goodisms, and religious doctrines that support assisting those in need.

Robert Lupton wrote in his book *Toxic Charity* about the issue of whether to help or not help. He points to the failure of a business-as-usual model when it comes to supporting the less fortunate. Lupton cited a Princeton University study reporting that 1.6 million American church members took short-term mission trips overseas in 2005, spending an average of eight days on trips at a cost of $2.4 billion.[1]

Lupton states his opinion that the number of such trips has increased every year since 2005, and these numbers do *not* include the weekday and weekend periodic mission trips that American church members take to our country's urban centers. Most short-term mission trips and projects do *not*:

- empower those being served,
- engender healthy cross-cultural relationships,
- improve the quality of life of the persons being served, or
- change the lives of the participants.[2]

Lupton wrote that, contrary to popular belief, most mission trips and service projects:

- weaken those being served,
- foster dishonest relationships,
- erode recipients' work ethic, and
- deepen dependency.[3]

I certainly do not lump all charitable efforts into the same basket—all charitable efforts are *not* created equal. There are many effective short-term mission activities in the United States, and I have no doubt that without the commitment to service of these organizations, our nation's poor would be in even worse shape. What I respect about Lupton's work is a focus on "holistic compassion" that calls for the establishment of "authentic parity between people of unequal power."[3]

We must ensure that our investments of time and money are yielding the results we want to accomplish as we meet the actual needs that others tell us they have.

Learning Holistic Compassion

Donald is a fifty-year-old white guy who has been homeless most of his life. He has a peaceful demeanor, and the love he has for the world shines brightly in his eyes. He moved into a homeless neighborhood on the banks of Buffalo Bayou in 2001. Houston's homeless community works a lot like any enfranchised community, complete with a form of government, commerce, entertainment, and friendships.

Donald and a friend decided to stop in at a live-music venue one evening, and there he saw something that shook his world. He saw what he described as "hippie girls" Hula-Hooping and expressing their artistic dancing without inhibition. He said, "That night me and my buddy decided to return to *our* art."

Donald told me, "I quit drawing when I was nineteen, and that part of my life disappeared—until it returned when I connected with a faith community where I was given a hot meal at the park. The group invited me to church, but I was reluctant to go because I had been taught that the church was really the devil."

I asked Donald how he had come to that conclusion about the church and found out that he had experienced "the church" as an institution with tremendous inconsistencies, hypocrisy, and judgment. In other words, no love in sight.

But Donald's perception of the church took a radical turn after an encounter with genuine *love*. He met six young women who were living in Houston and serving people. Much to his surprise, the women Donald met were familiar to him. He said, "I had sketched them from an image in my mind weeks before I ever saw them for the first time!"

When Donald met these young women, he said, "I was hooked on these people and their way of loving. I was amazed at the level of their commitment to serve the poor."

I count Donald as one of my close friends. He has helped me greatly in gaining an accurate perspective on homelessness and the life purpose of the homeless individual. He also has given me insight into the pain that dishonor can bring to human beings.

Talking with Donald is a little like sitting with a homeless guru. His experiences on the streets have shown him the best and worst in humanity. He knows what dishonor looks like from his perspective behind a cardboard sign. He said, "When I flew a sign on the street corners, it was the poorer people who helped me. I was puzzled by how unhappy many people look who appear to have so much. Protecting and maintaining status is a full-time job for them."

Donald speaks eloquently on classism in our society, the ways in which people fail to distinguish fear and judgment, and the struggle created by a failure to replace dishonor with honor.

Plain and simple, it was love that reminded Donald he was an artist and a person who was worthy of love. He once reflected, "Years ago the vessel [my life] broke and I had to decide what I was going to fill it back up with." Today, Donald is an accomplished artist and he helps Lanecia Rouse, program director of The Art Project, Houston, with art classes. This group, which meets on our church campus, is designed to empower and create self-sufficiency through the marketing of the students' creations.

Back to City Hall

What I came to see in the Houston ordinance issue was that the very things I value so highly in terms of food service were *not* being displayed by many charitable organizations.

In many cases, the food was adequate but not nutritionally excellent. In nearly all cases, no inspection was done to make sure the food was packaged in a safe way. I saw that it was a good idea to make sure the food being distributed to the homeless was truly *beneficial* to them.

I also came to see that ordinances limiting waste can be beneficial to the community as a whole. We are not called to honor *only* the homeless, but to honor *all* in our community. People who live close to feeding sites should not have to be left with excess trash or any disagreeable aspect of food-giveaway programs.

We are not called to honor *only* the homeless, but to honor *all* in our community.

Making the decision to honor other people—regardless of social, cultural, or economic differences—must be an intentional decision. We must *choose* to make it. We must have at the forefront of our thinking that we will seek to know what is best for others, and then choose to do what is best for others in the community where God has placed us.

Responding . . .

1. In what ways are you serving others in your church and in your community?
2. In your serving, how are you attempting to meet the actual needs of those being served?
3. In what ways are you showing honor to those you are serving?

CHAPTER 8

Love Creates Community

When we begin to reach out to others with unconditional love, we create community. An authentic, Christlike community is one that calls for all people involved to be loved, no matter their job, status, gender, class, or place of residence.

God has promised to help us in our charitable work as we strive to create a community of unconditional love: "Assuredly, I say to you, inasmuch as you did it to one of the least of these My brethren, you did it to Me" (Matthew 25:40 NKJV).

The Four C's of Community

I believe there are four main concepts involved in developing an atmosphere of genuine, loving community.

Compassion

It is impossible to honor someone for whom you have no compassion. It is even more difficult to create opportunity for that person if you do not have honor borne of compassion.

Our society today is marked by borderline narcissism at every turn. We are a me-first culture—we seek to do what is in our own best interests, often in blatantly disrespectful ways. The narcissist believes, "The world rightfully revolves around me." The narcissist routinely demands, "My way or the highway."

In a society of cultural narcissism, compassion is a game changer. Compassion declares, "Others matter."

In a society of cultural narcissism, compassion is a game changer. Compassion declares, "Others matter."

Compassion emits from deep within our spirits, and once it is uncorked, it becomes an unstoppable force. Compassion allows us to make connections with other people that lead to justice and mercy melding as one.

The biblical prophet Micah wrote:

He has shown you, O man, what is good;
And what does the Lord require of you,
But to do justly,
To love mercy,
And to walk humbly with your God? (Micah 6:8 NKJV)

To "do justly" means to place an emphasis on fairness or reasonableness in the way you treat people and make decisions.

To "love mercy" means to show compassion, kindness, or forgiveness to those over whom you have power.

When compassion is present, community is present.

Charity

I have discovered through the years that many people rush to help others without hammering out the details related to the long-term goals of what they are hoping to accomplish.

How many times have you watched a commercial that shows a homeless child and then asks for a financial contribution to help that child? The commercials work—people *do* rush to their phones to donate money to help homeless children. My question is always, "How many of those who are willing to give money are also willing to *do* something with their time and energy to help?" There's nothing wrong with giving money. But there's something much more right about establishing relationships with dislocated individuals so that you might give truth, mutual respect, and honor to those individuals.

Charity is not about you or about you feeling good about yourself. It's about creating community by working out the clear details involved in *serving* others.

Collaboration

As we reflect on the story of Jesus feeding the multitude, we notice that Jesus did not do all the work Himself. He gathered His disciples around Him and gave them full opportunity to help.

I believe Jesus did this for two main reasons. First, He was establishing a protocol for the way all of the work of the gospel was to be done. No human being is going to be able to do all that Jesus asks of him or her, alone. Spiritual community is the heart of Christianity. And what better way to experience community than by working together to help the needy?

I know other Christians in groups that minister to the homeless because I work with them in addressing the needs of the homeless. Their organizations and our Food Fair often collaborate to tackle specific needs. If people can't work together to help the needy, how can we possibly expect the needy to believe they are loved? Working together is a clear example of love in action.

If people can't work together to help the needy, how can we possibly expect the needy to believe they are loved?

Second, I believe Jesus called His disciples to participate and work together in His hillside feeding project because Jesus knew that helping the needy can be tiring. In war, the concept of *combat fatigue* refers to a weariness that comes when a soldier is constantly under attack. In acts of love and charity, there is a similar weariness that I call *compassion fatigue*. It comes when a person works constantly to meet the needs of others. Working alone, you can never have enough energy to do all that is required. If you do not have another person or group of people working alongside you, compassion fatigue can set in and wear you out to the point that you pull away from the project and never want to return.

God knows the physical toll our bodies and minds can handle, and He wants us to understand that it is acceptable in

His eyes for any person in a giving or service role to take periodic breaks. He wants us to work together in groups.

When we collaborate with others, it is easier for us to keep our eyes on the total need of a person or group of people we are serving. When one person in a group focuses on one need, another person focuses on another need . . . and so forth . . . over time and in a multitude of ways, the *entire* need can be addressed. One person cannot be everything to another person—in any dimension of life. We are called to work in community.

One person cannot be everything to another person—in any dimension of life. We are called to work in community.

Consistency

If there is one word that best describes God's relationship with His people, it is *consistency*. God's Word tells us that God never changes. "Yesterday, today, tomorrow, he's always totally himself" (Hebrews 13:8). He has promised never to leave us, to always take care of us, and to be quick to answer our prayers (Matthew 6:25–34; Matthew 28:20; Revelation 3:20).

We may think from time to time that we are alone or that God doesn't care. The truth, however, is that God never lets down any of His followers. He is always at work on their behalf. God is continually serving His creation, and He calls each of us to join Him in that endeavor.

Throughout His earthly ministry, Jesus showed consistency in living according to God's commands and purposes. He displayed a consistent love to His neighbors and fellow citizens. He never balked at those who requested His healing power. He never shooed away a person who sought out His wisdom. He never chose one person over another with favoritism. He was consistent in His service.

Consistency requires that we have a desire to serve and then a plan for serving. A plan becomes our benchmark against which we can evaluate our efforts and our achievements.

A person who helps out every once in a while is good, but usually the person who helps in this way does not have a life plan for service. The truly compassionate, caring, serving person has a goal to help in very specific ways—and to do so consistently and with a purpose that can be measured.

A Clear Motivation for Creating Community

As we create authentic, loving community, we must remember what is at stake in our service to other people.

- Are you serving for *your* sake or for their sake?
- Are you trying to help another person because that person has gone through all his options and you are what is left?
- Are you trying to help a person because you want some kind of "bonus points" applied to your account in your church or organization, or perhaps on a heavenly roster?

- Are you helping because somebody else told you that you *had* to help—with the result being that you are helping to ease the guilt another person has heaped on you, rather than from an inner motivation?

Those who serve with these motivations are serving *themselves*—seeking to meet their own emotional needs—more than they are serving others.

Make a Service Plan

There are several things a group, church, or charitable organization needs to do in developing a service plan.

State Specifically Whom You Intend to Serve

Pray about and then write down exactly who you plan to serve. Know the people who will be on the receiving end of your giving. Know their needs. What will be *most* helpful to them? Prioritize the needs you are addressing.

Define Yourselves as a Service Group

Be able to delineate the roles necessary for meeting your goals, and make sure you place individuals in roles that are suited to their talents and desires. If you fail to do this, people will quickly become inconsistent and unfocused.

Each of us is born with a unique set of skills and abilities. We do our best work when we are involved in tasks that call upon us to use our skills. Some people are planners. Others are not. Some people are reliable, steady, and good workers. Some are not. Some delight in being organized. Others enjoy being creatively spontaneous. My point is this: know yourself and know those with whom you are collaborating. Seek to fill all the roles necessary with people who are gifted in the specific roles to which they are assigned.

You will usually be able to tell fairly quickly whether people are genuinely committed to service. You will see it in their actions. You will see it when tough times come, when fatigue sets in, and when others around them disappoint in their degree of commitment. Align yourself with those who are genuinely committed, and seek to be a person who is firm in your own resolve.

Create Short-Term and Long-Term Goals of Service

As a group, create both short-term goals and long-term goals to which every person in the group can "sign on." In setting short-term goals, be sure to set specific times of service so that you allow for time off for those who are committed to helping.

Assign Costs to Your Goals

Look over your list of goals and then assign specific costs to each one—both in terms of financial resources and the resources of time. Keep the word *consistency* in mind. Only take on what you believe you can do consistently. Relationship is at stake!

Imagine you are opening a soup kitchen. You put up a sign in front of your church informing the community that from eleven o'clock in the morning to one o'clock in the afternoon on

Saturdays, you will offer a free meal to anyone who needs a meal. People come. You serve the food. They thank you, eat, and say, "See you next week." They aren't saying this because they expect never-ending handouts. They're saying this because they think a relationship has been established. A friendship now exists— perhaps only the faint outlines of a genuine friendship, but a friendly relationship nevertheless.

If you aren't open the following Saturday, that relationship is over. The people who have been fed are likely going to feel that they were just a "project" to you—and that no relationship was established. They will feel more dishonored by your inconsistency than if you never opened your doors to a meal in the first place.

Your commitment to service begins in the heart and must remain in the heart. It must be rekindled again and again *in the heart*. That commitment should not be based on what others do— how much they applaud your service or even how much they rely on or need your service. The commitment must be one that the *server* makes, and ultimately, the commitment is one between the person who serves and the Lord who served. Jesus never told His followers, "Stick with Me until you run out of food." Neither did He say, "Follow Me as long as you enjoy the journey."

Jesus loved and served people regardless of how they responded to Him after He had given them His best. He served people without always knowing them personally, extensively, or for a long period of time. He fed the people who had gathered on the mountain because they were committed to Him—at least for several days—and they were hungry.

When a group consistently provides what they have promised, they are displaying the highest form of commitment—and love. The total message of their lives is easier to hear and understand. A relationship becomes desirable. And in so many ways, Jesus becomes real.

When a group consistently provides what they have promised, they are displaying the highest form of commitment—and love.

Community Gives Rise to Hope

I have worked with the poor in Houston for twenty-one years. I have learned that a person's will to live can supersede adversity, struggle, and suffering, but the human will cannot thrive without hope.

I also recognize that we will always have the homeless in our midst. We will always have the poor among us (John 12:8). However, we do not need to accept *hopelessness*. We must continue to offer hope to those who are hungry, homeless, or in other types of need.

And finally, our hope must extend to offering help in a variety of ways that address the *whole* of a homeless person:

- We must reform drug policies.
- We must improve mental health care in our society.
- We must provide reentry therapy for veterans returning from military service.

- We must create employment opportunities and entre-preneurial training for people with felony convictions.
- We must build housing-first initiatives, which provide both housing and supportive services.
- We must change the "fair-housing" policies that make it impossible for a person with a felony to obtain housing.

All of these are ways to create community among those in need, and simultaneously to give them hope.

At the end of the day, if we want to create an authentic community, we must remember the following basic principles:

- Keep our commitments in our hearts.
- Stay consistent in our actions.
- Collaborate with others who are of like mind and heart, with whom we can work effectively.
- Be able to express our goals clearly.

In my personal life, I am moving toward implementing these principles in a way that truly builds people. As Christians, we ultimately are called to move beyond helping people to *building people* so that they might be able to help themselves and then serve others.

**As Christians, we ultimately are called
to move beyond helping people
to *building people* so that they might be able
to help themselves and then serve others.**

This does not negate the need to help or serve. Rather, it puts a new goal on the horizon—a goal that is extended by Jesus Himself. Our goal as Love Revolutionaries is to do our utmost to create a community that makes people whole.

Responding . . .

1. In what ways are you currently practicing the four *C*'s of community—compassion, clarity, collaboration, and consistency?

2. Do you have clearly stated definitions and goals related to those you are serving? If so, what are they? If not, take a moment to pray through and write out specific goals.

3. Is one of your foremost goals to develop a relationship with the people you are serving? If not, in what specific ways can you begin to make that your highest goal?

CHAPTER 9

Love Resists Anger

I am a coffee junkie. I drink at least three cups of coffee a day, and I have my favorite local coffee haunts in Houston. I frequent them often and on many days they function as my office. On even a slow day, I usually run into four or five people I know from St. John's. The coffee shops I frequent are alive with conversation, and people appear to be having genuine fun. Even the people who take my order and my money are cheerful and appreciative of my presence. I can't help but feel good while surrounded by accepting people in this environment.

In many ways, I enjoy coffee shops more than churches. At coffee shops, the greeters always seem cheerful, the staff and patrons are nonjudgmental, the atmosphere is conducive to conversation and friend making, and the product is usually good! Yes, I admit that I wish more churches were like coffee shops.

In the spring of 2012 I was hanging out at one of my favorite coffee shops when I saw a man I recognized walking outside the shop. He was a homeless person who frequently came to St. John's for a meal and who regularly attended our Sunday services. I went outside and called to him, "Hey, man! How's it going?"

He stopped and told me that everything was good. When I asked him to come inside the shop and have a cup of coffee with me, he agreed.

As I reached into my pocket to get out my wallet to pay for his cup of coffee, an irate coffee shop employee said, "You are not welcome here! Get out before I call the police!"

These two sentences sent me back forty years to the time of segregation in the South when blacks and whites could not eat in the same section of a restaurant. For a second, I thought the coffee shop employee was talking to me.

"Excuse me?" I said to the man. And at that moment, I realized he wasn't looking at me. He was glaring at my friend and pointing his finger at him. "He has to leave!" he said.

I looked behind me at my friend, who was looking down at his feet, understandably embarrassed. "Why does he have to leave?" I asked. "I'm paying for him."

"If he doesn't get out, I'm going to call the police," the man said.

My friend waved toward the door and suggested that we comply by leaving, but I wasn't about to do that. I had to know why. I pointed out that the last time I checked, we were in the United States of America and a shopkeeper could not deny a paying customer service without serious grounds for doing so. (No coffee pun intended.)

I bought coffee for my friend and then turned around and left the shop to take a seat outside with him. I was angry—very angry.

A longtime friend of mine was at the coffee shop and when he saw how angry I had become, he stepped in. "Reverend Rudy," he said, "you might not want to go there." He made me recognize squarely the impact my loveless response might have on the people in the coffee shop and on the reputation I had established in the area as a Love Revolutionary. Indeed, my words had not been spoken with love!

Ironically, this friend was a person I had first met twenty years ago, when he was a hungry, homeless teenager who ate dinner regularly at our meal program. He was now a successful businessman. He pulled me aside and explained to me privately that the man I had invited for a cup of coffee had been caught panhandling outside the coffee shop and had been asked to leave. After this friend talked with me, the manager of the coffee shop came from behind the counter and also told me the same story about panhandling.

I asked the manager, "What about the man's humanity?"

He responded, "I have a business to run. I'm not concerned about his humanity."

You can imagine—this entire encounter rubbed me raw. I felt that both my homeless friend and I had been assaulted, and rudely so. The coffee shop staff had reacted in anger, and I had reacted to them in anger. I left that coffee shop certain that I would never return.

Anger is an emotion I experience every once in a while. Like most people, I get angry for many reasons, some of them unjustified and some of them seemingly justified.

I'd like to think my eruptions of anger are always justified, but in truth, I know that God's Word calls us to shun red-hot rage and to refuse to harbor anger in our hearts. The fact that I still feel anger welling up in me as I recall this incident tells me—and you—that I'm harboring anger.

So what am I, and other Love Revolutionaries, to do with our anger?

Two Types of Anger

Unjustified anger is anger that has no legs to stand on. It is the anger of a child who starts to pout and the pouting only makes matters worse because the adults generally start to laugh at his pouting!

Unjustified anger usually results in public embarrassment. It leads to nothing being solved or resolved.

God's Word says that anger is acceptable as long as it doesn't lead to sin. The apostle Paul wrote, "In your anger do not sin" (Ephesians 4:26 NIV). What does that mean? It means that there is a type of anger that is *justified*. It means that anger can and should lead us to pursue justice, but it must never lead us to behavior that alienates others from God or damages our own relationship with God.

In short, anger is the emotion God has given us to *compel* us to seek justice. If your anger isn't pushing you to seek justice for the righting of a wrong, repent of your anger and make efforts to get rid of it.

What Makes Us Angry?

Through the years, I have counseled and conversed with hundreds of people, and I have concluded there are four basic causes of anger at work in all of us to some extent or degree, pretty much all of the time.

Uncommunicated Standards

One of the prime causes for anger is rooted in our expectation that we should all be expert mind readers! Too often a leader will have high expectations for the performance of those following him or her, and when that performance is not given, the leader will become angry. That happens in the business world, in most professions, and in the church too.

Imagine that you are a new student in a high school, terrified of everything around you, and in one of your classes, you walk into a classroom as the teacher is taking roll. When your name is called you raise your hand . . . only to have the teacher shout at you and tell you never to do that again.

What did you do wrong? You don't have a clue. Raise your hand? Walk in after roll was being called? Admit your name? Sit in a chair you shouldn't have occupied? You likely will go through the rest of the day in a daze, dreading ever going back to that classroom. There was some kind of expectation that you did not fulfill. But that expectation was not communicated to you, so the net result is likely to be unresolved anger—from both the teacher's side and your side.

How often does that same scenario, or a similar one, play out in our institutions, families, and world at large? This failure to communicate sets up premeditated resentment. The most basic dictum of good communication states that we must be clear about the response we desire to our communication.

**We must be clear about the response
we desire to our communication.**

Unappreciated Performance

Another cause of deep anger is related to something about our performance in life that goes without applause or appreciation. People can get angry when others aren't impressed with them in the way they believe others should be! This story is as old as Cain and Abel, told in Genesis 4. Both brothers brought sacrifices to God: Cain's sacrifice was some of his produce, while Abel's was the choicest lamb in his flock. God favored Abel's sacrifice and not Cain's. Cain's reaction was one of anger—in fact, extreme anger that Cain was not willing to release, which ultimately became anger that led him to kill his brother. Cain had acted in a way that he thought would impress God, and God not only failed to applaud or appreciate what Cain had done, but He registered His disappointment to Cain.

How often have you performed your tasks at work and received no reward or even simple recognition for doing a good job?

How often have you resented a spouse for failing to appreciate your hard work?

How often have you volunteered to go the extra mile and received no attention from a superior?

I've been there too. I often work hard on accomplishing projects and writing sermons and building facilities and training teams of people—and the vast majority of the time, no one mentions what I've accomplished or am working hard to accomplish. A lack of applause or appreciation could make me angry. I choose not to let it!

Dr. Robert McGee wrote a book titled *The Search for Significance*, in which he details the downfalls of an addiction to success. Those who are continually in search of applause often find themselves in the "performance trap," which Dr. McGee describes as, "I must meet certain standards in order to feel good about myself."[1] Even if others fail to applaud their efforts, they are determined to applaud themselves. The net result is often a deep fear of failure, a striving for perfection, and an inner drive to succeed that can lead them to manipulating others or withdrawing from all situations that might have a risk of failure. Those who are caught in the performance trap manifest very high degrees of anger, resentment, pride, and depression, as well as low self-motivation over time.

The answer to this dilemma is to overcome the performance trap by grace through faith in God. The apostle Paul said it this way: "Therefore, since we have been justified through faith, we have peace with God through our Lord Jesus Christ" (Romans 5:1 NIV).

Check your motivations for your actions. Are you motivated to love and serve others because of praise you expect to receive? If so, find a better motive.

Pursue acts of love that you believe will build your relationship with God and others, apart from any act of appraisal or approval. You'll likely find that you are less angry the longer you focus your efforts on relationships rather than performances.

Pursue acts of love that you believe will build your relationship with God and others, apart from any act of appraisal or approval.

Unexpected Behavior

A third major cause of anger can come when we feel surprised by an unexpected circumstance or turn of events. This unexpected behavior may also involve a misunderstanding of another person's behavior—perhaps an assignment of evil intent even in cases where no evil exists.

To a degree, that's what happened at the coffee shop. The manager and employee in the shop assumed that my homeless friend had entered the shop to panhandle again. They didn't take the time to see that he was with me, nor did they factor in that I was paying for his coffee of my own free will. In fact, I had *offered* to treat him to a cup of coffee. His appearance in the shop was unexpected behavior to the manager and employee, and it was not perceived accurately.

A great deal of anger related to unexpected behavior seems to be rooted in cross-cultural misunderstandings. For example, in Japan, businessmen don't shake hands when greeting each other. They bow instead. Here in the United States, if a businessman extends his hand to a Japanese businessman, the American *expects* a return extension so the two might shake hands. When that doesn't happen, misunderstandings can arise in both the American and the Japanese man.

The best way to avoid this type of anger is to develop patience. Choose *not* to react too quickly in any type of provocative situation. Take time to analyze what is happening. Give other people the benefit of the doubt—in many cases, the other person is *not* trying to insult you or provoke you.

The owners of the coffee shop lost income that day because they jumped to a conclusion too quickly! Remember, genuine love is not rooted in fear.

Unmatched Plans

Anger can also be manifested when we assume that our own plan for our lives is identical to God's plan for our lives. When we discover that God might have a different idea, we tend to erupt in anger and call God "unfair" and "unkind."

An Old Testament prophet named Jonah had that kind of anger. Jonah expected God to desire the annihilation of the

Assyrians, the number-one enemy of Jonah's people. Instead, God commanded Jonah to go to Nineveh, the capital city of the Assyrians, and call the people to repentance. Jonah did not want to go to his enemies, and he most assuredly did not want to deliver a message of God's forgiveness to them! He rebelled, and you likely know the rest of the story. Jonah was thrown overboard, and when he finally agreed to do God's bidding, he ended up in the belly of a great fish especially prepared for him. The fish suffered a serious bout of indigestion, vomited Jonah on the beach, and from there, Jonah walked many miles to Nineveh and delivered God's message. Jonah, however, remained angry. Nothing about God's plan lined up with what Jonah thought God *should* do.

One of the prayers I pray often—even after many years in ministry—is this: "God, whatever it is You want me to do, open up every door You want me to walk through and close every door that's not Your best for me." Sometimes God answers that prayer in ways that I like, and sometimes He doesn't. Sometimes He tells me to do things I feel totally unprepared for. Sometimes He makes it very clear that He will help me do His bidding, with both of us—God and me—knowing that I am totally incapable of any success apart from His help. In nearly all cases, I find I can look back and say that God's plan was better than any plan I could ever have made.

"God, whatever it is You want me to do, open up every door You want me to walk through and close every door that's not Your best for me."

What Should Prompt
a Response of Anger?

Anger is a human emotion that compels us to seek justice. What, then, are some of the situations or circumstances that warrant a response of justified anger?

I grew up keenly aware of Rosa Parks. A hardworking black woman, Rosa was riding home on a bus that had a white section and a black section. When a white man got on the bus and could not find a seat in the white section, the bus driver asked Rosa to move to the back of the bus so the white man could take her seat, which was in the first row of the "black section." Rosa refused to move, and as a result, she was expelled from the bus and arrested for failure to comply with the driver's wishes. Her action helped catapult the civil rights movement in the United States into high gear. Rosa had taken a stand for justice. Her one-woman-sized anger was far more potent than she realized at the time.

More recently, a girl named Malala Yousafzai experienced injustice. She spoke out against the work of the Taliban in her nation of Pakistan. At a young age, she saw it as a heinous act of injustice that the Taliban was closing schools attended by girls and forbidding the education of girls and young women. The Taliban retaliated by shooting her with the intent to kill. Malala survived the attack and was helped by surgeons in the United Kingdom. Since that incident, she has spoken out with a maturity far beyond her years and has become one of the most influential people in Pakistan.

Malala, like Rosa Parks, was angry at an injustice. She voiced her anger in a blog that circled the globe. Others became angry at the injustice of her situation. And in the end, Malala became a champion for girls in many other nations beyond Pakistan.

Jesus was even angry at times. In fact, there are several instances in His ministry in which He manifested anger at a deep level. In each case, Jesus was angry at an injustice or a disregard for the holiness of God.

His response was not to appeal to various political or religious authorities. Instead, Jesus appealed to His followers to take action against injustice by a most unusual means: forgiveness. He reminded others of a loving God who desired to forgive them *as they forgive those who had wronged them.* A major message of Jesus was this: "Judge not, and you shall not be judged. . . . Forgive, and you will be forgiven" (Luke 6:37 NKJV).

Jesus appealed to His followers to take action against injustice by a most unusual means: forgiveness.

A right is something that is due to all people. A privilege is something we must earn. When we become angry at injustice related to basic human rights, we can count on God being on our side, enabling us to have influence and to protest against those injustices without sinning. However, when we become angry in support of privileges that we desire, we must be very careful. Those expressions of anger are not likely to elicit God's support or the support of others over time.

What Rosa, Malala, and Jesus All Knew

Oppressed, marginalized people who are receiving harsh treatment often need someone outside their situation to help them. There may very well be things that God asks you to do on behalf of those who are experiencing an injustice miles away from where you are located, including people of different race or ethnicity. Don't be surprised! The anger kindled in you at injustice is meant to find an outlet that is both godly and effective.

Sometimes the best responses are ones that make little sense to us, and they might even bring us discomfort. God sometimes asks people to turn the other cheek (Matthew 5:39). In other words, get hit a second time if that's what it takes to call a larger number of people to their senses. God might ask you to give away your coat—as well as your shirt (Matthew 5:40). If that is what it takes to call people to see the injustice of failing to meet the basic needs of the poor—in this case their need of clothing—then so be it. God may ask you to go the extra mile (Matthew 5:41). If that's what it takes to keep the unjust from trampling on the just, do it!

God will never ask you to *do* evil. Rather, He will ask you to oppose evil without mirroring it. Look for God to challenge you to:

- Seize the moral initiative (the high ground).
- Find a creative alternative to violence.
- Assert your own humanity and dignity as a person.
- Meet force with gentleness or humor.
- Break the cycle of humiliation.
- Refuse to accept the inferior position.

- Expose the injustice of the system.

- Take control of the power dynamic.

- Force powerful people to make decisions.

- Respectfully stand your ground.

- Recognize your own power.

- Be willing to suffer rather than retaliate.

- Cause the oppressor to see you in a new light.

- Deprive an oppressor of a situation in which a show of force might be effective.

- Be willing to undergo the penalty for breaking unjust laws.

- Die to fear of the old order and its rules.

Jesus admonished His followers not to react violently against those who are evil (Matthew 5:39). He also told them to be "wise as serpents and harmless as doves" (Matthew 10:16 NKJV). One of the main principles of nonviolence states, "Power is not only what you have, but what your enemy thinks you have."

God will never ask you to *do* evil.
Rather, He will ask you to oppose
evil without mirroring it.

Be creative in your expressions of anger that confront injustice!

Be Aware of Microaggression

One of my daughters recently received a master's degree in clinical psychology. She introduced me to a term that is something I have experienced much of my life; I just didn't have a name for it. The term is *microaggression*.

Microaggression is anger expressed in subtle, bite-sized pieces—exemplified in everyday life by demeaning and degrading terms, veiled insults, and covert attacks rooted in stereotypes (usually about race, class, gender, ability, status, and orientation). Microaggressive people often send these messages:

- You do not belong among us.
- You are abnormal.
- You are not trustworthy.
- You [in your stereotype class] are all the same.

Dr. Derald Wing Sue, author of *Microaggressions in Everyday Life: Race, Gender, and Sexual Orientation*, says, "It is reported that Maya Angelou has likened racial microaggressions or petty humiliations to 'small murders' in contrast to the blatant forms of oppressions called 'grand executions.'"[2] Microaggression kills something in the human spirit—a little bit at a time.

Let me assure you that microaggression is not limited to any one ethnic or racial group. It exists worldwide and is a two-way street between many cultures and races.

One of the major challenges facing the church today is overcoming microaggressive attitudes, statements, and behaviors. Microaggression and genuine love cannot coexist.

Microaggression and genuine love cannot coexist.

Too often people believe that if they aren't doing anything overtly hateful or evil, then they are likely doing something that is at least partially loving and good. That isn't necessarily so! Love is overt, intentional, and behavioral. It is recognizable. The absence of microaggression is neutrality, not love. Don't err in this. You lack of participation in something ungodly does not mean you are godly!

Responding to an Angry World

Unlike the vow I took as a child, I now choose *not* to be angry. And in the place of anger, I choose to love. I choose to treat people with fairness and equity.

Whenever possible, I will confront injustice—and do so once I have cooled off a bit so my words can be heard clearly.

After my experience at the coffee shop, I got together with several people and we began to create a business that would welcome anyone in the community who has been turned away from other places. I got people involved who know coffee and food. I challenged the group to excellence. And I helped establish a goal that we would not only make a fair profit, but we would show unconditional love, without anger, in the way the business was conducted. Trust me—I can hardly wait for this business to open so I can go there frequently and become a regular customer!

I challenge you today to let go of debilitating, unjustified anger. Instead, use righteous anger to motivate you toward a higher and greater good—something aimed at righting a wrong and bringing an unjust situation to an end.

As you deal with your anger, always make sure you are interacting with God. Make an effort to see things the way God sees things and to respond as you believe Jesus would respond. Let your anger stay within the parameters of love that keep you in relationship with others.

Let go of debilitating, unjustified anger.
Instead, use righteous anger to motivate you
toward a higher and greater good.

When in doubt about whether to register anger or to demonstrate love . . . choose love.

Responding . . .

1. What makes you angry?
2. In what ways do you tend to display your anger?
3. Have you had good success in letting go of anger so it doesn't turn into bitterness, resentment, or hate? If so, what did you do? If not, what do you *wish* you could have done?
4. Describe a situation in which you were motivated by anger to take on an injustice that you knew that God would like to see remedied. What happened?

CHAPTER 10

Love Avoids Materialistic Pursuits

I have a great friend named Craig Bowie. He attends St. John's and is one of the most prolific and talented artists I have ever known.

When you meet Craig, you'll undoubtedly notice that he wears an eye patch over his left eye. When he comes to trust you, he may show you what the patch is covering. You'll see that he has a damaged eye, and the damage is part of a scar that runs down his face.

Craig is a great example of the truth that our past experiences often leave scars—physical, mental, emotional, or spiritual. Even so, our scars do not define us.

Craig was born in San Antonio and grew up a Texan. When he was young, some of his friends introduced him to drugs. By seventh grade, he was familiar with weed and pills, and a little later, dope. Craig's father had died, and smoking dope seemed like a good idea—it eased the pain of losing his father and helped him forget his problems. Drugs soon became a fixture in Craig's life, and the more he used them, the more he wanted them. To use drugs like this, of course, requires a lot of money. Craig had some checks from his father's social security benefits, but that wasn't enough. His parents had bought him a horse and given him riding lessons as a child, and as Craig's need for drugs increased, he began to sell his saddles, and eventually, his horse.

Craig met Janice, or JJ as many people in her neighborhood called her, at a concert after he had gone through all his money and resources. JJ worked as a prostitute. She told him how she wasn't a big fan of her current pimp. Seeing a window of opportunity, Craig offered his services as JJ's pimp. How hard could being a pimp be? You stand on a corner and take people's money and then you spend it on dope. He thought he might have to beat up a few people here and there, and maybe break a few bones, but overall, he saw the outcome as worth that cost.

Although he was threatened by JJ's former pimp, Craig stuck to his plan and became one of the best-known pimps in the Galveston area. Pimping JJ led to more girls coming to him for his services, and after a while, he had several regular girls he took care of in exchange for a cut of their money. Taking care of the prostitutes usually meant keeping an eye on the men who wanted their services, protecting the girls from johns who tried to rough them up, and making certain the money was paid before any services were rendered. It seemed to be a perfect setup. While the girls were servicing the johns, Craig was off with his cut of money to find his dope dealer.

The job of pimp means that you have to fend off two sets of enemies—johns who don't pay, and other pimps who want to steal your prostitutes. One day, that became very clear to Craig. One of his friends said, "Hey, Craig, isn't that your girl walking into that house over there with that other pimp?" Sure enough, that's what was happening. Craig raced after the girl and the pimp, and when she didn't open the door to the room where he believed she was working, he kicked down the door and faced the prostitute—who was holding a shotgun. She fired before Craig could get out of the way, and he was hit directly in his left eye. He fell backward as his world went black.

Love Is PIMP-Proof

Craig was not a pimp because he wanted to be a criminal. In many ways he was like many people in our society who are seeking power, money, and, on a deeper level, love and appreciation. In this chapter, I will use the acronym PIMP to mean *Person Indulged in Materialistic Pursuits.*

Those who are in pursuit of material gain rarely consider the potential costs of their pursuit. They rarely face the potential significance of the pain and suffering they might experience.

At the core of a Person Indulged in Materialistic Pursuits is the self-focused question, "What can you do for me?" The PIMP is not only in pursuit of money or material goods, but in control over people. PIMPs are nearly always manipulative and out to use people even more than they use things.

The only way truly to avoid becoming a PIMP is to pursue a relationship with the One who created you. It is only then that you can fully comprehend that you are more than your stuff and give up seeking to control other people.

The only way truly to avoid becoming
a PIMP is to pursue a relationship with
the One who created you.

The Bible tells about a man named Jacob who stole his way to the top. Jacob tricked his brother to buy his brother's birthright. Then he tricked his father to get his father's blessing that was meant for Jacob's brother. His brother sought to kill him, so he ran away to his uncle's home, where he worked for more than fourteen years to gain two wives. When Jacob finally decided to return to his home, he found himself alone in the wilderness one night and had a wrestling match with God. Instead of God handing Jacob the death sentence he deserved for trying to deceive and manipulate everyone he had ever known, God changed Jacob's nature! Genesis 32 describes how God turned Jacob from a deceiver into a true believer.

Is that how *you* would have treated Jacob?

Consider Craig. How would you have treated *him*?

Many people in the Christian world would rather turn their backs on people like Jacob and Craig than give them the time of day. They don't want to associate with people who are shady or who have a criminal background. Rather than reach out to these people to embrace them with the love of God, Christian people often seek to dishonor them and to distance themselves from them.

But how does God *want* us to great the Craigs and Jacobs of this world?

With *love. Period.*

We face a big challenge in that. The key is to forgive criminals and do our best to restore them to a community where they can have a positive life. We fight crime, not because we dislike the people who commit crimes but so that others can avoid the pain and suffering that go along with crime. We fight crime with the power that builds lives: *love.*

We must stop keeping score against others and start taking action. If we are honest with ourselves, we will face the truth that there is a fine line between those who keep the law and those who don't. I often tell people that the only reason I don't have a criminal record is because I didn't get caught. I suspect the same is true for you—in some way, at some time, you have been a Person Indulged in Materialistic Pursuits!

**We must stop keeping score against others
and start taking action.**

Loving Churches Help Others

One way we can PIMP-proof our communities is for churches to take an active role in strengthening one another. I believe strongly in the need for churches that are economically enfranchised to work with churches in the parts of a city that are economically disenfranchised. Men and women in more affluent communities can do many things to help—from providing childcare or after-school programs, to mentoring students, to teaching English—all of which helps young people to see that hard work *can* produce a different life.

Providing Mentoring and Education

Churches can develop educational programs for both children and adults. Most economically enfranchised churches have dozens of members with professional backgrounds and positions. These people can become valuable mentors when they offer their skills and information in evening or weekend classes.

Stanley Phill came to St. John's as a crack-addicted high-school dropout. Through the ministry of our church, he not only learned to read, but he also obtained a high-school equivalence diploma. Today, he is a college graduate and runs a successful nonprofit organization that has developed millions of dollars of affordable housing projects inhabited by people with HIV/AIDS. Stan is a shining example of what can happen when a community decides to pursue a solution rather than avoid a problem.

Providing Upwardly Mobile Clothing

Another way to foster job opportunities for adults in impoverished communities is to hold clothing drives. I noticed years ago that many people in our community were capable of holding higher-income jobs, but they were afraid to seek them out because of their wardrobe. They thought, *I'll be turned away the second I walk through the door because I don't have a suit.*

They were probably right. We live in a world that makes instant judgments on the basis of appearance. So why not help people by providing quality clothing for them as they pursue better jobs? If clothes make the man, as the saying goes, then Christians can help others in a highly significant way by donating some of the suits or dresses they aren't wearing anymore. It is remarkable how a change of clothing can help change a person's outlook and self-esteem.

Welcoming Released Prisoners

Several years ago I realized that a large percentage of the people who were attending St. John's had prison records. So we developed an outreach to area inmates through visitations to prisons, and we welcomed these individuals to our church after they had served their prison sentences. The ministry is called the Path to Freedom, and it is led by a young professor, Dr. Jonathan Chism, who likely has never even had a traffic ticket in his life!

Jonathan's passion for released prisoners—or as he calls them, "returning citizens"—has created a community of people who seek to understand the plight of former inmates and help them move beyond judgment to acceptance. This group meets every Monday evening. Sometimes as few as fifty people are in attendance, sometimes up to seventy-five. The men and women come together to support, share, and welcome new "returnees" to the free world. They are also given shoes, clothes, job referrals, and cell phones.

There are many things that churches can do to help those who are coming out of prison:

- Maintain halfway houses where returning citizens can stay while they get back on their feet and find jobs.

- Provide a haven for women who are trying to escape from human trafficking—a haven where they can develop new skills and enter career fields that are rewarding and fulfilling to them.

- Put together consortiums of businessmen who can provide returning citizens with jobs so they can begin to earn their way in places that also provide mentoring and spiritual support to them.

We in the church *can* be the leading edge in rehabilitation—if we only choose to be!

We in the church *can* be the leading edge in rehabilitation—if we only choose to be!

Providing Rehabilitative Hope

Often when I talk to churches and organizations about poverty and ways we can help people, I run into a wall of opposition that boils down to this line of argument: "These men and women had the opportunity to make a choice in their life. They made the wrong choice."

I am always amazed that the same people posing this line of argument are quick to say that Jesus was sent to earth to give us a second chance we didn't deserve, so we would not have to suffer an eternity separated from God.

It is our responsibility to extend second chances to as many people as we can—even if we don't think they *deserve* a second chance. When we choose to offer second chances, we spread love. And in nearly all the cases I know, an atmosphere of love opens a person's heart to the possibility of God's love and forgiveness.

It is our responsibility to extend second chances to as many people as we can—even if we don't think they *deserve* a second chance.

Every person has a history.

Every person has made mistakes.

Every person needs someone to hold out hope to him or her.

Every person is in need of forgiveness and a second chance.

And the good news is this: every person can be a source of *love—period!*

Providing a Platform for a Future

Many people return to a life of crime after being released from prison for one simple reason: they don't see a future for themselves apart from the life they knew in crime. They can't even imagine a better way to live.

Beyond hope, we need to provide specific pathways for former inmates to develop a new future that does not include criminal associations and activities. Note that word *associations*. Those who are returning citizens need new relationships. They need new friends. They need people to whom they can turn for sound advice and emotional support.

There are countless ways Christians can organize ourselves to provide ongoing support groups for people who are returning to society after prison. The key is for us to *choose* to become actively involved in some way with others—not holding up the former prisoners' mistakes before them but rather wiping the slate clean and giving them the emotional support they need to create a new life for themselves. It is a way of saying, "I forgive you." And that is a way of saying, "I choose to *love. Period.*"

We must be quick to say to those who are trying to turn away from dealing drugs, prostitution, pimping, and robbery: "The church doors are open for you. We'll do our best to help you walk through them. We have hope that you can make it!" And then, if a person falters, what do we do? We continue to help. We continue to cheer them from the sidelines.

After the Shotgun Blast

What happened to my friend Craig? Obviously, Craig did not die from the shotgun blast to his face, though he did lose sight in his left eye. After a stint in the hospital, he managed to clean up his life for a few years. He began working for others by teaching in a community center for kids. He learned how to write grants so that the community center could receive money and get more tools to help the children.

And then Craig slid off the track. In 1996, he began to use drugs again and fell down a sharp hill of despair until he had a fight with a man who had assaulted him earlier. Craig landed in jail, and it was there in jail that he came back to God.

As a child, Craig's grandmother had taken him to church and had taught him to memorize Bible verses. One of his favorite passages as a boy had been Psalm 16:1–3. His grandmother had given him this passage to memorize after several neighborhood boys had beaten him up.

That night in jail, Craig began to wrestle with God. He asked God why He had forgotten him. He felt totally powerless. And then he remembered and began to speak aloud the psalm he had memorized when he was seven years old:

> Preserve me, O God, for in You I put my trust.
> O my soul, you have said to the LORD,
> "You are my Lord,
> My goodness is nothing apart from You."
> As for the saints who are on the earth,
> "They are the excellent ones, in whom is all my
>   delight." (Psalm 16:1–3 NKJV)

The next morning, Craig's cellmate asked him why he was in jail. Craig told his story and his cellmate gave him the phone number of a man who might help him. This man was someone who promoted second chances in life. Craig called the man, and the man listened to Craig's story and offered to help him. He bailed Craig out of jail and helped him with various court-related issues.

Craig returned to Galveston, where he had a dream about a place he would end up clean and sober. He didn't know where the place was located, but he knew from his dream what it looked like! He also knew that if he stayed in Galveston, he would keep getting into trouble.

Craig asked his wife to drive him to a drug rehabilitation center in Houston. When he arrived, he did not have the proper identification to stay at the center. So he called his nephew for help—a nephew who happened to be an associate pastor at St. John's. His nephew, Michael, told him about our Resurrection House transitional living facility. When he walked through the doors of Resurrection House, he was floored. It was the place he had dreamed about the night after his court appearances! Craig knew he was in the place God had for him. Resurrection House, by the way, is a remodeled building—it was formerly the motel my dad and I once owned and operated.

Craig began treatment for his drug addiction and faced other problems in his life. He grew closer to God. He has now been clean and sober for more than nine years.

I like telling Craig's story because he represents what many Christians go through. You may have struggles that are very different from Craig's, but nonetheless, your struggles have nearly destroyed your life. Everybody either is a problem or is living with a problem. Perhaps you have moved away from God's purposes . . . but God has not given up on you. You can find acceptance in God's house and become a part of God's family. Yes, it is possible.

The apostle Paul wrote to the Corinthians, "[Love] doesn't keep score of the sins of others" (1 Corinthians 13:5). That challenge is given to each of us today as well. We are to *love. Period.* Love without conditions means looking at what can be done today, not what was done yesterday. As Craig often says, "Yesterday is yesterday, tomorrow is another day, but today is a gift."

When God forgives you and me, He wipes the slate clean and puts our past in the past. God not only forgives us, but He *forgets* what we have done. God puts people squarely in the present. And it is there, in the present, that we can make a fresh start toward a new future.

It isn't easy to forgive. It isn't easy to move beyond the past. But it's the right thing to do.

Today Craig runs Public, Inc., a nonprofit company involved in providing affordable housing. He is an accomplished and successful artist. He's also a good friend who is a source of hope and encouragement to everyone he encounters.

He is a product of *love. Period.*

Responding . . .

1. "Everybody either is a problem or is living with a problem." How do you respond to that statement?
2. What difference does hope make in your ability to work through life's problems?
3. How might extending love to another person help that person face and overcome problems?

CHAPTER 11

Love Overcomes Evil

One of the scariest experiences as a parent is teaching a child to drive. You are not only worried about your child's safety, but you are worried about your own safety! When you sit in the passenger's seat as your daughter or son takes the wheel and heads out onto the open road, you can't help but feel your legs tense up and brace for a crash. When your child makes a left turn across oncoming traffic, or comes a little too close to the bumper in front of you, you can't help but see your life flashing before your eyes. Then you take a deep breath and realize you are still alive.

Parents of older children also know that you never really let go of the fear of your child driving. Every time my daughters, both of whom have been driving for a long time now, back out of the driveway, I feel a tinge of anxiety. *Will they be okay? God, please keep them safe!* I have to trust God that at the end of the day, my daughters will pull back into the driveway. There's nothing I can do about it except to pray.

Driving lessons are the way I've started this chapter because the car has always been an important part of our family life.

From the time our daughters, Morgan and Ryan, were very young, many of our most important family discussions have taken place in the car. We have eaten meals in the car and helped with homework in the car. Like millions of American families who commute and spend many hours a day in their vehicles, we are a car-connected family.

Ryan is the younger of my two daughters. In many ways, she is a lot like her mother. She is intelligent, kind, hardworking, and expects a great deal from herself. She's a natural-born leader.

Ryan and Juanita were in the car one day when Ryan burst into tears. Juanita asked what was wrong, and Ryan told her she hadn't been feeling well for a long time. She felt depressed and anxious and didn't know why. Later that night, Juanita and I agreed that the best thing for Ryan was for her to see a therapist. We knew something was happening inside Ryan, but we had no idea what.

For several weeks, Ryan saw her therapist regularly. At first, the sessions involved the usual stuff. She talked about school and family and various things in her life that were creating pressure inside her.

I went on about my days as though everything was normal. I decided that Ryan would be just fine—she just needed someone outside the family to talk to. But then one day, Juanita and I were called to a meeting with her counselor. Ryan was there as well, and it was clear she was nervous.

The counselor said that Ryan had something she wanted to tell me. My mind spun. *Oh no, what's wrong!*

Ryan took a deep breath and blurted out, "I was molested."

Suddenly I couldn't breathe. Nothing I had thought could possibly have been as bad as what I had just heard. "What?" I finally asked.

Tears were welling up in my daughter's eyes and suddenly they flowed like Niagara Falls. "I was molested when I was younger," she said.

"When?" I asked.

"When I was four years old."

The room went black for me. Blood rushed to my head and I felt as if my heart shattered into a million pieces.

I couldn't begin to tell Ryan's story better than she can tell it, so I'll let her share it with you:

There are so many words that a smile can't say. The truth is, you don't get asked many questions when you are smiling. I learned that very early on and thus, I wore my smile like a mask.

I was four years old when someone I thought was safe violated my body and my trust. I knew even then that the news of what had happened would break my parents' hearts. Even at four, I wanted to protect them from my pain.

It's amazing what your brain can do to protect itself from tragedy that it's not ready to comprehend. I knew what happened was wrong. But somehow I thought I had done something to deserve what happened to me. I couldn't face the pain of my parents' knowing, so I stuffed the pain deep inside. I knew my smile would never clue them in. I knew if I smiled they wouldn't ask any questions. So at the tender age of four, I started smiling.

I smiled my way through the sadness. In my four-year-old mind, what happened had occurred because I was "such a pretty girl." From that point on, I tried to make myself invisible. I didn't want to be pretty.

All my work to make myself invisible was in vain. Being chubbier than the other kids made me an easy target for jokes. My academic abilities made me the perpetual teacher's pet, which certainly did not make things better for me with my peers. Some people say that always being picked last, and enduring countless playground taunts, are character-building experiences. I only knew that I kept asking, "Why me?"

Grown-up and transformed, I now see it all through a different lens. It's hard to champion the cause of an underdog if you've never been in that position, but championing others comes naturally for me now because even on my best day, I can still see my little-girl face in the mirror and relive the pain.

Holding in pain is not easy. My pain frequently leaked out in the form of unprovoked tears. I had emotional skin as thin as tissue paper. I couldn't take a joke. I cried at the slightest reprimand. Among those I loved, I was regarded as sensitive. What nobody knew was that I was carrying a burden much too big for me to bear.

After a few years, I didn't want to be invisible any longer. I wanted to be a pretty girl again. But it wasn't as easy to reclaim beauty as it had been to discard it. I worked my way onto the honor roll, the spelling bee, and volleyball team, and I joined the cheerleading squad. I started figure skating and hosted a slumber party. I kept smiling and doing my best to hold all my emotions together on the inside.

I was eleven years old when things started to fall apart. My math teacher pulled me aside one day to let me know that my almost-perfect grades in her class were falling. I chuckled and she replied that my grades were no laughing matter. She didn't know I was chuckling to keep from crying.

I remember getting a large glass out of the kitchen cabinet, filling it with water, and then reaching for a bottle of pills. I had heard that people could overdose on pills, so I figured surely a whole bottle would do. I sat in front of my computer trying to compose the letter I wanted to write to explain my actions to the ones I loved. I didn't want them to think my choice to end my life was their fault.

And then, a thought came to me—it was a moment of grace that convinced the eleven-year-old me that the end was not *then*. It was not my first moment of grace. That had come years before when, in the midst of the violation, God seemed to cover and protect my spirit. I knew He was protecting the spiritual me.

Shortly after my near-suicide attempt, my paternal grandfather was given a terminal diagnosis. My mom decided that my sister and I needed to talk to therapists to process our feelings of grief, and although it would be six more years before I truly began to work with a therapist regularly, that encounter with counseling started me on a journey to wholeness.

Fast-forward to tenth grade. I was captain of the cheerleading squad. I had a strong grade-point average and was on track to go to my dream college. Yet in the midst of all the external good, I felt like I was dying inside. I couldn't bring myself to tell anyone about my pain until one Sunday in September. I told my parents for the first time that I was feeling depressed. It was like a valve opened inside me. It was the first time I was able to voice what was happening deep inside me, and the release felt good.

In the fall of my senior year of high school, I was working on getting my driver's license. I was driving on the freeway with my mom in the passenger seat. I was attempting to make a lane change when the driver in my blind spot suddenly honked loudly. I was so rattled by the near miss that I broke down in tears. Even though we arrived safely at our destination, I was inconsolable.

Mom tried to comfort me but eventually gave me some space to myself. I felt totally out of control. Coming that close to a wreck had brought back the feelings of being out of control and part of a "wreck" that I had felt thirteen years earlier. I faced for the first time in many years *why* I was having the feelings I had, why I was always on the verge of crying, why I was so sensitive, why I wanted to die. It took a few more weeks before I could work up the courage to tell my parents. They were as devastated as I had thought they would be. But I knew I needed to give voice to what had happened to me. Before I told Dad, however, I made him promise that he wouldn't kill the man who had violated me. I didn't want my father to go to prison for murder or attempted murder!

The year after I shared the news of my molestation with my parents was filled with ups and downs. I had a lot of feelings to work through. I was angry on so many levels and for so many reasons. I went three states away to start college, hoping the distance would help. In the spring of my sophomore year, I finally acted on what a number of people had suggested: I filed an official police report. That act lifted the dark, heavy curtain of shame just long enough for me to catch a glimpse of freedom's light.

Filing a complaint consisted of me sitting in a room with a detective and a video camera, recalling every detail I could remember about that horrible night. My parents had joked through the years about my amazing memory for details, and for once, my detailed memory served me well. I have no idea how long I was in the room with that detective, how many tears were shed, or how many questions were asked. I swore with my right hand raised that I would tell the truth, and I did. I walked out of the room feeling as if a huge load had been lifted from my shoulders.

I had a conversation with a female deputy shortly after that, and she informed me that the man who had violated me would be charged with a felony count of aggravated sexual assault of a minor. She also told me that while the case would be investigated to confirm the details of my report, it would be difficult to bring about a conviction for an event that had happened so many years ago. She did say, however, that if the case proceeded to a grand jury, that would be a good sign.

The months that followed were filled with anxiety. Periodically I'd get a call with an update from the assistant district attorney handling the case. I threw myself into my premed studies and prepared to spend six weeks in the northeastern part of the United States at a prestigious medical school. I ended up leaving the program after only two weeks, though, recognizing that I needed to resolve this issue from my past before I could fully engage in my future.

In September, I got a call I never hoped to get. The case had finally gone to a grand jury. But despite my testimony, they moved to have the case dismissed. My mom gave me the news and said the assistant district attorney had said she was very sorry things had turned out as they did. During my phone conversation with Mom, the tears started to fall. I did not regret my decision—filing the police report had helped me reclaim a piece of myself that I had thought was lost. Now I needed to make peace with the way things ended. That took some time, but the peace eventually did come.

Through the years, I had asked, "Where is God?" on a number of occasions. One time as I was feeling angry and in despair, I suddenly "saw" God's loving arms shielding and protecting my mind, soul, and spirit in the midst of the devastation to my body. I realized that while I had been injured and thrust into pain, I had not been irreparably harmed! I didn't die. I didn't melt away into a pool of nothingness. God had enabled me to continue to live and to progress in life. I even began to see that God had used, and would continue to use, this evil assault against my life to strengthen me, refine me, and give me an ability to savor life's beauty and joy in a way that many people never experience.

The darker an encounter with evil is, the joy of the Lord is just that much brighter.

As disappointing as it was to experience a failure in the human justice system, the clearer it has become that God's justice *will* prevail in God's own timing and methods.

As big as an obstacle might be, God's ability to heal is bigger.

More Real than Evil

My daughter Ryan's experience with evil created a new aware-ness in me that God's love is *more real* than the reality of the worst evil.

God's love is *more real* than
the reality of the worst evil.

Both Juanita and I have had several encounters with evil. One of the most profound encounters occurred during our third year of ministry. We were having dinner at one of our favorite restaurants, a place where we ate at least once a week.

We had just placed our order when a woman in a long black dress walked by our table on her way to the restroom. Juanita and I looked at her, smiled, and greeted her. The woman smiled back, nodded, and continued on her way to the restroom. Within seconds, we heard grotesque sounds of someone vomiting and then moaning as if in great pain. After what felt like several minutes, the sounds finally ended. The room was completely silent. The woman never came out of the restroom! We were perplexed and I finally suggested that Juanita go check on the woman, and she did. She returned to our table with a confused look on her face, saying, "There is no one in the restroom, and there are no windows or back doors."

When the waiter came back to our table we asked if he had seen the woman in another section of the restaurant. He had a puzzled expression as he said, "You two are the only customers in the restaurant, and there are no back entrances to the restroom."

We both had seen this woman and spoken to her. Then we reached the same conclusion—we had experienced an encounter with evil. There have been other times when evil has paid us a visit to keep us off balance or stop something that God has authorized, but neither Juanita nor I had an awareness that evil had paid our daughter a visit when she was four.

What happened to our daughter was not a vision or an apparition. It was *real*. Ryan was victimized by someone she knew and trusted, and she was not able to stop the molestation from happening. One of the hardest truths I have ever faced was my realization that I, her father, had not been able to prevent the molestation, and I had not been present to help my daughter. For more than a decade, I had not discerned the pain Ryan had experienced, and I had been unable to help heal it.

No one in our family was capable of preventing what happened back then. And none of us is capable of destroying the haunting memories that still rise from time to time.

Ryan was correct in saying that she feared I would kill the man who had violated her. I certainly was angry enough to do that. Even now, murderous thoughts can flash through my mind when I think of him, and I come face-to-face with the truth that grace is extremely difficult! God's call is for me to forgive this man, to release him from my mind and heart, and to trust God to deal with him. Vengeance is not mine to exact (Romans 12:19).

Hatred and withholding forgiveness will harm me far more than my hatred and lack of forgiveness will hurt him.

But how can I forgive this man? How on earth can I refrain from throttling him and smashing his face into the ground? How am I to refrain from acting on my anger?

I find myself coming back to what the apostle Paul wrote: "Love does not delight in evil but rejoices with the truth" (1 Corinthians 13:6 NIV). It is up to me to choose to focus on the truth and power of God's love, rather than to dwell on the fact of one man's evil deed. I must choose to *love. Period.*

**It is up to me to choose to focus on
the truth and power of God's love, rather than
to dwell on the fact of one man's evil deed.
I must choose to *love. Period.***

How Do We Respond to Evil?

I have learned that there are three things God calls us to do to be set free from a preoccupation with evil.

Focus on the Victim

When I first heard that my daughter had been molested, all I could think about was the man who had violated her. I wanted to rip his head from his body. My daughter may have felt suicidal in the aftermath of her experience, but I felt homicidal. My therapist finally helped me realize that homicide and suicide are opposite extremes of the same polemic experience.

I was so caught up in my anger that I almost lost sight of how much I needed to reach out to my daughter with tender love, comfort, and care. I needed to invite Ryan to tell me about this horrific experience, without her worrying that I would erupt in anger. I needed to be there to help her in her pain. I was finally able to get to that point, but I want to encourage you to take action far sooner than I did. If someone comes to you with a story of violation or suffering, don't ignore their need and think about your own reaction or about the perpetrator. Focus your energy on the needs of the victim. Stay in close contact with your own feelings and choose to allow love to become the most powerful feeling inside you.

The apostle Paul wrote, "Bear one another's burdens, and so fulfill the law of Christ" (Galatians 6:2 NKJV). The "law of Christ" is the law of love. The way we fulfill God's command to *love—period*—is to willingly take on the pain and suffering of the one who is hurting. We must take on *their* burden, not manufacture our own burden of hurt. How do we do this? We listen to the person. We cry with the person. We sit in silence with the person. We pray with the person. We encourage the person—not with platitudes, but with the truth of God's love and tender mercy.

**The way we fulfill God's command
to *love—period*—is to willingly take on
the pain and suffering of the one who is hurting.**

In the end, I know the burden is one that only Ryan can carry with God's help. But I also know that it can be my role to remind her that God is there to help her, and so am I, in any way she can use my help. One of the wisest things I did was to ask Ryan, "How can I help you?" I had to accept her answer as the right answer.

Allow Yourself Time to Reflect

The psalmist wrote:

> I waited patiently for the Lord;
> And He inclined to me,
> And heard my cry. (Psalm 40:1 NKJV)

This psalm speaks volumes to me about the feelings we have when we come face-to-face with suffering—both our own suffering and the suffering of others. We all tend to ask, "Where was God? Why did God let this happen?"

The answers are never simple, and in many cases, we will never receive an adequate answer to our questions. But we can know that God always has a purpose, and He always provides a way for us to move beyond suffering to genuine hope. The questions we are wise to ask are these: "What do You want me to learn from this, Lord?" and, "What is Your plan for me moving forward? How can I get beyond this pain and experience Your hope, joy, and loving presence again?"

We must be patient to put our minds and emotions at rest long enough to get to God's answers, which can lead us to a stronger and more peaceful state.

When I became patient, that helped Ryan to be patient. She needed time to process her own questions, to explore her faith, and to ask God to reveal His guidance to her. In the process, she discovered strength she didn't know she had. She experienced tremendous mental and spiritual preparation for what God has for her in her future.

Put the Matter in God's Hands

As much as I wanted to take matters of justice into my own hands, I learned to place the person who had hurt my daughter in the hands of God. There really is nobody who can exact justice the way God can!

There really is nobody who can exact justice the way God can!

A couple of years ago, I was stopped at a traffic light, and a man started to cross the street in front of my big truck. Who was this man? You guessed it. It was the man who had molested Ryan.

I struggled to keep my foot on the brake pedal. The man never noticed me.

I called Ryan and said, "Guess who just walked in front of my truck?"

She said without hesitation, "I know who, and the fact that you are talking to me and not to the police tells me he is still walking."

Then Ryan said something that stuck in my mind like a thumbtack on a map: "That's good, Dad, because I would have hated to have lost twice."

Boom! Those were just the words I needed to hear.

When we take matters into our own hands, we are robbing people in our lives from seeing God's grace in action. If I had given in to the revenge and rage I felt in my own heart, how could I ever have looked into the eyes of my daughter and convinced her that God can heal our pain, disappointment, and anger? Forgiveness—in my case, taking the man out of the angry clutches of my heart and putting him into the hands of God—is the only thing that gives full opportunity for God to teach His greatest lessons about grace and mercy.

Forgiveness . . . is the only thing that gives full opportunity for God to teach His greatest lessons about grace and mercy.

Ryan is trusting God that things will turn out to her good. I must do the same.

Ryan is a testimony of God's grace at work. I trust that in my keeping my foot on the brake, I am a testimony of God's grace to her.

The Church's Role in Overcoming Evil

I am fully convinced that issues related to molestation, rape, and other forms of abuse and violation need to be addressed in the church openly and candidly. These are acts of evil, and we must denounce them as evil. Those in the church must be trained to speak words of comfort to victims, manifest patience as both victim and comforters seek God's direction, and then take appropriate steps to see that justice is done. If we ignore the reality of sexual crimes, the church will lose its credibility in addressing other forms of evil.

My daughter's story is one of triumph. No one in our family is happy that the man who molested her walks free, but we do have joy that God has used this experience to refine and cultivate Ryan. She savors God with deep appreciation, and she fully embraces life's joyful moments. Ryan is now in medical school and working toward making this world a better place. She sees what happened to her as a lesson in how to help others and how to be sensitive to those in pain.

Ryan said to me not long ago, "I see the bad in a whole new light. No obstacle can compare to what I have overcome. I know that even on my darkest day there is still joy to be found."

The church has a role to play in applauding the grace of God in the lives of those who are facing and overcoming abuse and assault. Once again, it is love that lifts up the wounded person. It is love that heals and makes whole.

Responding . . .

1. Various statistics about abuse, rape, and molestation tell us that one in three adult women in our nation has been the victim of sexual assault. That includes women in the

church. Are you one of those victims? If so, how are you experiencing God's love and grace? Are you married to one of those victims, or are you in close relationship with a victim? If so, how are you helping that person come to forgiveness and wholeness?

2. Many people in our world today are taught that evil does not truly exist—it is just a misunderstanding and the result of bad childhood experiences. What is your response to that way of thinking?

3. In what ways do you believe God is equipping you—or might equip you—to confront evil whenever you find it walking across your path?

4. Have you ever struggled to keep from taking vengeance and justice into your own hands? What did you do? What was the outcome? Why do you think God's command to forgive is so difficult for us to follow?

CHAPTER 12

Love, Truth, and Friendship

At some point in our lives, we are wise to ask, "What is a good friend? And am I one?"

Some people regard friends as those who have your back. Others say friends are those who cheer you up when you're down. For me, a friend is someone who will be honest with me—even if that means telling me things I don't like to hear.

I've had many true friends through the years, and the common factor in our friendships is that my friends want to help me grow as much as I want to help them grow. Friendship is meant to foster personal growth—to help us become all that we can be according to God's design.

Friendship is meant to foster personal growth—
to help us become all that we can be
according to God's design.

The Bible has a number of stories in which two people challenge each other for the purpose of spiritual development. We can read about Elijah and Elisha, Ruth and Naomi, and Paul and Timothy. But have you stopped to consider the relationship between King David and the prophet Nathan? It was Nathan who confronted David about his sin of adultery with the wife of one of his top soldiers, and the subsequent order from David that led to this soldier's certain death. It was Nathan who confronted David despite the fact that David could order him to be killed. Nathan loved and served God as a faithful prophet. And Nathan loved and served David as a faithful citizen. Nathan *had* to speak truth to David. Love and loyalty to God and to David required him to do so.

The same goes for us. We cannot love without conditions—and then refuse to speak the truth.

**We cannot love without conditions—
and then refuse to speak the truth.**

The Cost of Truth-Telling

Jonathan Gregory and his wife, Connie, attended St. John's on our first Sunday worship service, and they joined the church that day. Soon after, in September 1992, we began serving the homeless community one hot meal a week, and that quickly became three meals a week. Jonathan has told me on several occasions through the years that it wasn't the church that attracted him; it was the people in it and God's presence in them. God's presence made him want to work for God at St. John's—and work he has done! He resigned from his job and began to volunteer full time.

Jonathan and Connie soon began to lead the feeding ministry, and they gathered a group of incredible people to work alongside them. They used their little red Chevy pickup truck to haul cooked chickens from a nearby grocery store several times a week. They loaned the church their credit card to cover expenses when the church account didn't have sufficient funds for food. They developed and manifested a tremendous heart for the poor.

Jonathan created our mission statement for the church, which says:

> Our mission is to restore hope, faith, and love to the entire community; and remove the barriers of classism, sexism, and racism from the worship experience. Our mission is realized through an array of ministries that promote universal recovery in a warm, compassionate, Spirit-filled, and Christ-centered environment.

The meal that our church was serving to the homeless at the time Jonathan arrived on the St. John's campus was not the greatest meal. Jonathan referred to it as "serving slop to our homeless friends." He pulled me aside one day and said, "Rudy, we shouldn't feed people food we wouldn't eat, and we shouldn't give them clothes we wouldn't wear." That day was a turning point for our ministry.

Jonathan was a man who wanted *more* for the poor, not just the bare minimum. He began organizing our money better so we could supplement the food that was donated with food we bought. He reached an agreement with a local grocery store down the road, took a certification course so he could oversee the kitchen, and did everything in his power to provide the best possible meals to the fifteen hundred people we served.

He also began organizing renovation projects around the church and advanced the funding of those projects, again using his personal credit card on occasion. The building of St. John's was eighty-five years old at that time, and it was in dire need of repair.

Jonathan was a banker, so he frequently paved the way for us to get the best financing possible to refurbish and update the church facilities. He worked with local businesses to support the food kitchen, worked with banks to arrange loans, and kept records of our accounts so that we could survive even the closest scrutiny from auditors. He kept an eye on the church finances without receiving any salary.

I don't think Jonathan ever saw himself as serving the church. He was serving God, and it just happened that he was serving God through serving St. John's.

As Jonathan become more and more devoted to serving in our church's homeless ministry, he came to me one day with great concern. He said, "Rudy, we need to talk."

I thought something was terribly wrong—perhaps our finances were messed up or we didn't have sufficient funds to pay for food in the kitchen.

"What is it?" I asked, worried.

He said, "You haven't been giving money to the church."

I calmed down. "Oh," I said. "Yes, I know."

"Why aren't you?"

"Well, Jonathan," I began to explain, "I'm giving so much more than just money to the church. I'm giving my time and energy. I have made tremendous financial sacrifices to be in ministry and to serve this church."

My words only made Jonathan angry. "What do you mean? Do you think you're sacrificing more than others?"

I looked at him as if he had lost his mind. "Jonathan, are you kidding me?"

And that's when I could tell he was *really* angry.

He told me bluntly, "You're not making any more sacrifices that anyone else at this church. If you can't give, then I can't work with you. You aren't exempt from showing God your love through your giving."

The conversation ended and he walked out.

I was angry after he left. A few minutes passed and then I felt God calling me to reflect on what Jonathan had said. I began thinking about things from Jonathan's perspective, and I had a much clearer understanding about why Jonathan had said what he said. He truly was a friend. He loved me enough to confront me.

Jonathan had not come looking for conflict when he realized I was not giving to the church. He had come to confront me out of love for God and for me. His intent was simple. He wanted to make sure that I was practicing what I preached. Jonathan was willing to risk our friendship by confronting me in an area where he felt I was misinterpreting my call and purpose. That's a friend! That's *love. Period.*

Active Love in Friendship

There are several concepts that are vital to the way we express love in friendship.

Speak from Knowledge

Jonathan's confrontation of me came from a place of knowledge. He was our church's financial manager, and he knew who was giving what. He also knew that what he was saying to me was right before God. Jonathan loves God with his whole heart, and he knows that the heart of a church is God—a pastor does not make a church. God's love and those in the church who love God are what make worship genuine and allow a church to thrive.

I had developed an attitude that I was making the church by the force of my love, leadership, and personal devotion. Jonathan knew better. It was God who was making the church. So Jonathan came to remind me of my place in the grand scheme of things. I am a servant doing God's work, but others at St. John's are also servants doing God's work. I was not the only one commissioned to love and serve, or to use my faith. I was not exempt from God's commands related to financial giving.

I needed to hear what Jonathan said. And I knew I was hearing words that were flowing from God's wisdom.

One of the first lessons I learned while contemplating Christianity as a member of Windsor Village in Houston, Texas, was that "every member is a minister." We each are responsible for being the hands, feet, eyes, ears, and heart of Jesus.

We each are in need of friends who will remind us of these truths. We need friends who will remind us that we are human and make mistakes—and at the same time, love us and help us. We need friends who remind us not to be haughty or proud—and at the same time, encourage us and build us up to love and serve God with greater intensity and effectiveness. We need friends who will remind us, "Hey, you're no different from anyone else. We're all called, but in different ways"—and at the same time, help us develop our unique skills and fulfill our specific roles.

**We need friends who will remind us that
we are human and make mistakes—
and at the same time, love us and help us.**

We need friends who will *love us. Period.*

Christ Is the Center of the Concern

If you are going to confront someone about something she is doing or not doing, make sure the focus of your conversation is on Christ and His message. Jonathan spoke to me in a way that was clearly God's word to me.

Jonathan wasn't as concerned about the money I wasn't giving as he was about my disobedience to God's Word. In the book of Deuteronomy, God reminds us that giving isn't a burden we must bear; it is a celebration of God's love for us:

> Give freely and spontaneously. Don't have a stingy heart. The way you handle matters like this triggers

GOD, your God's, blessing in everything you do, all your work and ventures. There are always going to be poor and needy people among you. So I command you: Always be generous, open purse and hands, give to your neighbors in trouble, your poor and hurting neighbors. (Deuteronomy 15:10–11)

Giving is a matter of obedience, but obeying God should never be burdensome! Obedience is the way we express our love to God and receive His love in return. We cannot fully love God without obeying Him (1 John 5:3). And when we give to God and His kingdom work, we will be blessed as much as those who are receiving our gifts.

When we give to God and His kingdom work, we will be blessed as much as those who are receiving our gifts.

In confronting me, Jonathan was focused on my relationship with God, far more so than on our relationship with each other. I believe he even would have been willing to sacrifice our friendship in order to bring me back into a closer relationship with God. Now that's a friend who *loves—period*!

If your criticism of a friend is rooted in him not doing something *you* want him to do or not do, think again. If your friend is truly doing what God desires, you likely are off base in your criticism. If your friend is not doing what God desires, make that your focus.

Make Sure Love Is in Your Heart

We need to recognize that anger and love often spring from the same place. That's why we are deeply hurt when we are on the receiving end of anger from people we deeply love. Anger is often an expression of deep concern or deep care.

I have no doubt that my friend Jonathan was motivated to confront me because he loved God, loved St. John's, and loved me. A triple dose of love is hard to resist! He wasn't angry out of greed or out of a legalistic concern related to tithing. He wanted me to receive the best of God's blessings and love, and to give God the best of my love and devotion.

Jonathan didn't confront me to damage our friendship or shame me in any way. His desire was for our relationship to endure, to be strong, and for us to continue to work together with a passionate concern for ministry. Even in his anger—and in my subsequent anger—love was the strong foundation underneath both of us.

Love Is Giving

Giving is one of the most delicate subjects related to the church. I believe this is because most people do not fully understand what the Bible teaches about money. They see only examples of financial misuse and abuse, and they react negatively any time the words *stewardship* or *giving* pop up in the context of church.

The truth is, the operational definition for loving is *giving*. The most famous verse in all the Bible says, "For God so loved the world that He *gave* His only begotten Son, that whoever believes in Him should not perish but have everlasting life" (John 3:16 NKJV; emphasis added).

Those who love deeply cannot help but give. Those who give generously nearly always do so from a heart of love.

Those who give generously nearly always do so from a heart of love.

How do we show our love to God? We show our love by giving—by giving our worship, our time, our talents, our energy, our devotion, our thanksgiving, our praise, our adoration, our money, our resources, our influence. Anything of value is something worthy of *giving to God!*

Giving is our response to God's gift of grace—our sign of gratitude for all God does and is. When it comes to giving to the church, I encourage you to consider the following:

- View the offering as a time of worship—see yourself as giving to invest in building God's kingdom and supporting ministries that transform lives.

- Take a Christian financial management course or a Bible study that emphasizes financial principles from a biblical perspective. Learn how God regards money.

- Write a "money autobiography." Take note of the times and seasons in which you gave the most, and those in which you were blessed the most. You are likely to find them to be one and the same!

Recognize that the goal of giving to the church is not the mere giving of your money—although as Jonathan accurately stated to me, money is a necessary manifestation of our love. God wants all of you. He doesn't just want a portion of you, or a portion of your love and devotion. He wants it all. Indeed, He is worthy of it all!

God wants all of you. He doesn't just want a portion of you, or a portion of your love and devotion. He wants it all.

God desires for us to love Him to the degree that we will do whatever He asks us to do—and give whatever He asks us to give—for as long as He asks us to do it!

Jonathan lived that out. He worked with us at St. John's until he realized that he was no longer needed as a church administrator. He found a replacement for that position and then assumed a new role in the church as a Bible study teacher. As he transitioned from one role to the next, I saw him do what he has done throughout our friendship: he asked God where God wanted him next.

Almost simultaneously with his decision to transition away from being church administrator, Jonathan received a call from the bank where he had worked before he became a volunteer on staff at St. John's. They offered him his old position—his old office, even his old phone number—but at a huge increase in salary. Jonathan felt it was a clear message that God was about to use him in a new way, and this big increase with a steady paycheck could be used for the sake of spreading God's message in new ways.

God has rewarded Jonathan and his wife in another way—after twenty years of marriage, praying and believing that they might be parents one day—they got a call saying that a child was available for immediate adoption. It was the fastest adoption I have ever witnessed. Within a month, they brought home a baby boy.

Love is always God's highest and best blessing to us.

Love must always be our highest and best act of giving to God.

**Love must always be our highest
and best act of giving to God.**

Love must be the highest and best motivation for our friendships—not just some of the time, but all of the time. Not just in the good times, but in the times when speaking the truth is the most loving thing we can do.

Love and truth go together. Always.

Responding . . .

1. How do you feel when someone gives to you with extreme generosity? Do you feel love? How do you feel when you give generously to others?

2. Have you ever confronted a friend out of a concern for your friend's highest and best relationship with God? What happened? Was your confrontation permeated with love?

3. Who is demonstrating love toward you by helping you grow spiritually? Who are you helping?

Moving Forward in Love

Melvin Gray is one of the most active congregants at St. John's. He is the president of the board of The Bread of Life, our food outreach program that also provides life-supporting services to the homeless community in Houston. He also helps lead Sunday worship services.

Melvin is one of the kindest people I have ever met. His folksy, outgoing personality makes him easy to talk to, and he's also one of the smartest people I know.

Melvin is one of the more noticeable people at St. John's because he's well over six feet tall . . . and white. His business card gives you a glimpse into who he really is. It reads: "Fool for Christ, friend, listener, poet, and occasional snake handler." I personally do not share Melvin's love for snakes, but we are all entitled to our uniqueness!

Melvin and I often introduce ourselves to others as brothers. Our introduction is usually met with a curious stare, until we add, "We have the same Father."

St. John's is not a church concerned with someone's race, but we are still a predominantly African American gathering. However, Melvin did not let that reality affect his choice of a place to worship. He has told people on more than one occasion, "I needed a place more about grace than disgrace. St. John's provides that." Those who hear this are often puzzled. What could cause this soft-spoken man to deserve disgrace? What could anyone hold against him?

Like each of us, Melvin has a history. Things he has told me about himself are reasons many churches would probably turn Melvin away and ask him to stop volunteering on their behalf. Melvin, however, looked for a church where personal failures do not negate worthiness or value in God's eyes, and I'm glad he found what he was looking for at St. John's.

Melvin's Journey of Faith

Melvin grew up in segregated Mississippi, where he easily could have developed stereotypical opinions about African Americans. He attended an all-white school and went to an all-white church. He then went to a private university where he completed an undergraduate degree in biology. While there, he experienced an overwhelming call to enter the ministry and became a priest. Melvin had a stable life with a wife and two children for nearly three decades—but then, after twenty-eight years of marriage, his wife moved out. A year later, during their separation, the leaders of the church where he was a priest asked him to resign because they didn't believe he was performing at the level he once had.

After another year of doubt and pain, including divorce, he reentered pastoral ministry at another church. He was welcomed in this new community and protected by the church's leadership. He felt that the church had his back and that he was valued and loved. It was there that Melvin met a woman who was a member of his congregation and who was also going through a divorce. She turned to Melvin for counseling and emotional support, and they began to see a lot of each other despite the fact that she was still legally married. Melvin will be the first to admit this was a mistake; he knew they were crossing moral and ethical boundaries. He moved to another congregation in another state, and the relationship came to an end when the woman decided to reconcile with her husband. Unfortunately, she and her husband then united in a plot to see Melvin removed from ordained ministry.

Melvin knew his offense was grievous, but he did not believe that one mistake in thirty-one years of active ministry should warrant his resignation. The day came, however, when Melvin was asked to resign from the priesthood. Ashamed, tired of fighting, and ill advised, he signed the document that requested his resignation. A combination of humiliation and blind loyalty to the institutional church had left him very easy to manipulate.

Melvin was told he needed to leave the church immediately, with no opportunity to say good-bye, so in 2008, he found himself outside the church, with no other clergy talking to him, a failed marriage, and an inappropriate relationship on his ledger of sins.

Emotionally down and relationally out, Melvin decided to move to Houston, where his children and a grandchild lived. For a while, he stayed away from all churches, but the pull of God was insistent. He began searching for a new spiritual home, afraid of being disgraced again, but also making no attempt to hide his past or allow himself to be marginalized.

I had met Melvin fifteen years before he moved to St. John's, and we became friends. We had remained in touch, off and on, over the years. He called me after he moved to Houston to tell me he was going to give St. John's a try. He came to the church and remained.

In one of my early encounters with Melvin, years before he came to St. John's, he admitted to me that he had not cried—not a single tear—in thirty years. I was blown away at that, because I cry often and freely. Melvin said he could not cry. I told him to tell me when he finally did cry because I was afraid of the flood of emotions that might erupt if those bottled-up tears ever found his tear ducts.

Three years after Melvin resigned his last clergy position, he attended our noon worship service. The choir began to sing, and then, all of a sudden, I saw Melvin Gray begin to cry . . . uncontrollably. He fell on the floor and cried and cried and cried. Juanita and I stood on either side of him to make sure he had privacy to cry for as long as he needed to cry. At the end of the service, I stepped to the platform and told those gathered, "My friend Melvin has just cried for the first time in more than thirty years." The congregation vocalized their support of him, and Melvin has been crying ever since.

Melvin is a prime example of a person who has used events and experiences in his life as stepping-stones rather than obstacles. He knows what it means for God to strengthen us and to walk with us through the darkest valley of disappointment. He knows with certainty that God never gives up on us.

Comfort for Those Who Don't Think They Can Persevere

Although the details of Melvin's journey are distinctive, he is not unlike hundreds of people I have met who grew up in church and then left the church because, for one reason or another, they were turned off by what they witnessed or felt. Even so, these people continue to feel the tug of God on their hearts, and they continue to believe in God in spite of their lack of a spiritual home.

Many are like Melvin—they don't give up on God or church but keep hoping and searching for a place where they will be accepted and find authentic love and hope. Others, however, do give up—on God, on themselves, and on church. If you have given up on church or on God, Melvin's story has a strong message to you.

Expect Your Faith to Be Tested

I believe that a faith that hasn't been tested is a faith that can't be trusted.

A faith that hasn't been tested is a faith that can't be trusted.

Even pastors struggle with their faith from time to time. What we put out seems to fall short of what we receive as input. We grow weary of criticism, judgment, and lukewarm hearts in those to whom we are trying our best to impart a passion for God. We reach a place where we say, "Lord, I can't take it anymore." We want to quit. But God says, *I'll help you.*

If we can move beyond that discouragement and receive the renewing strength of God, we often look back on that experience and say, "I was tested, but God helped me overcome." We begin to see our problems or issues in light of the overall journey God has set us on.

I do not believe that God puts problems in our path. But I do believe that every life's journey *has* problems in the path. That's simply the nature of life in a fallen world, living with broken people. God calls us to learn from those problems, work through those problems with faith, and then move forward on our faith journey with greater strength and deeper conviction. God does not *give* us trouble, but He does help us overcome trouble.

God does not *give* us trouble,
but He does help us overcome trouble.

The apostle Paul wrote, "Do not be conformed to this world, but be transformed by the renewing of your mind, that you may prove what is that good and acceptable and perfect will of God" (Romans 12:2 NKJV). In every act of transformation, we will find a degree of brokenness and pain. This is an opportunity for us to prove what is:

- "good"—the right things from God's perspective for all mankind;
- "acceptable"—the right way to live according to God's plan and purpose for us; and
- "perfect"—the best choices to make in order to experience God's favor.

You and I will never face a test that others have not faced. The purpose of a test is for us to learn from it, pass the test, and apply the lessons we have learned to new situations. The tests of life that we go through also become a platform for us to help others who are experiencing their own tests!

When we see others around us who are experiencing troubles, we must not shun them or shy away from their issues. We need to remind them that they are facing a faith test, and then do what we can do to help them address that test and pass it!

Sometimes We Have to Leave in Order to Get Somewhere

People leave churches today with far greater frequency than most pastors care to acknowledge. Some leave because they become bored. Some are no longer challenged to grow spiritually. Some leave because they move to a new city or state.

During the past two decades of my ministry at St. John's, more than eighteen thousand people have joined us, but thousands of others have moved on for a number of reasons. That's a difficult thing to accept as a pastor, but I have discovered that the vast majority of those who leave our church are not leaving because God told them to leave. They are leaving because they have not fully engaged in active ministry at St. John's. They often are looking for the church to spoon-feed them all things necessary for spiritual maturity, without any active participation on their part.

From my perspective, many people fail to get the full benefit of their church experience for two main reasons: they are passive observers more than active ministers to others, and they fail to see that others around them have amazing faith stories that can help them grow in their ability to believe that "all things are possible" with God (Matthew 19:26 NKJV).

Still others, like Melvin, are pressured to leave the church in a cloud of rejection and accusation. Those departures are especially difficult.

I watched Melvin take hesitant steps after he joined St. John's. He had to learn how to live without the encumbrances of what others had always expected him to be. He had to learn to live without fear that others were continually judging his every move. Melvin also had to learn how to be part of a church with a different worship style than he was used to.

Melvin finally reached the place where he realized that God had called him to *leave* virtually everything about his past, except his beloved children and grandchild, in order for him to *receive* all that God wanted him to have.

Melvin stumbled and fumbled occasionally . . . but he never gave up. He is an example to me of the person described in Proverbs 24:16: "A righteous man may fall seven times and rise again" (NKJV).

Perseverance produces strength. Each time you fall and rise again, you are stronger.

If you are abandoned by your church, rejected in a marriage or other relationship, or are lost in a new city, give yourself time to heal from the sharp wounds you have experienced, and then get up and ask God, "What do You have for me now?" When God shows you a step to take—even if you are a bit uncertain and think it might only be a step to *try*—get up and go in that direction. Ask God to guide you step by step until you arrive *fully* at the place He wants you to be. It's there that He has a plan for you to grow and develop.

Give yourself time to heal from the sharp wounds you have experienced, and then get up and ask God, "What do You have for me now?"

You Are Never Alone in the Race

The Bible tells us, "Since we are surrounded by so great a cloud of witnesses, let us lay aside every weight, and the sin which so easily ensnares us, and let us run with endurance the race that is set before us" (Hebrews 12:1 NKJV). You may not have any friends or supporters in this life, but even if that is the case—which it rarely is—you can look to others who lived victorious lives and draw courage from their example. There is always someone who can come along and share your journey.

There is always someone who can come along and share your journey.

Knowing that others are firmly and consistently persevering on a faith journey with you is tremendously comforting! It gives you freedom to be your authentic self. It gives you hope that your personal mistakes and flaws will not produce rejection. It gives you an ability to focus on God, more than on yourself or on the ways others are treating you.

The more Melvin gave God a chance and gave others in the church a chance, the more he was willing to extend chances to others. Love became cyclical. Melvin had love for God and others renewed in him, and as a result, others poured an increasing amount of love into his parched soul.

How a Church Can Enable Perseverance

There are three things I believe every church can do to help people persevere—not only in their church attendance, but more importantly, in their faith.

Remember Who Is Ultimately in Charge

We tend to get weary when we think that we are in charge of all outcomes—or of even a few outcomes! Jesus made it very clear that all forms of loving ministry are done because He commands it and also enables it. Jesus leads us into ministry, and He is with us at all points of our loving, giving, teaching, preaching, giving, worshipping, and ministering.

Jesus said to His followers:

> All authority has been given to Me in heaven and on earth. Go therefore and make disciples of all the nations, baptizing them in the name of the Father and of the Son and of the Holy Spirit, teaching them to observe all things that I have commanded you; and lo, I am with you always, even to the end of the age. (Matthew 28:18–20 NKJV)

Jesus issues this challenge to you and me, and then He says, *I'm in this with you.* We are never abandoned to isolated or "solo flight" leadership.

This is not only true for pastors, but for every person who is actively engaged in seeking to help others and to love them unconditionally. When we *love—period—*we serve others as guides, not as judges, jury members, or executioners.

We Must Practice Our Faith, not Pontificate

People learn the most from watching how other people act, including how they speak, when and where they show up, and how their deeds and words match up. We learn from those we call role models—those who are living out the way we *want* to live, which is generally how we believe God wants us to live. This is true for every person in the church, not just a pastor or leader.

We need to spend more time, I believe, in studying how Jesus lived. He celebrated the gifts and talents of people. He admired simple acts of faith. He continually called His followers to acts of forgiveness and restoration, not to specific tasks or the establishing of appearances. He cared far more about a person's current relationship with God than about anything in his or her past. He loved people in their humanity and He allowed for personal differences. He always pointed to his heavenly Father as the source of all healing and wholeness.

We must do the same—not by preaching on a corner, but by living on the pathways the life that Jesus modeled.

We Must Never Ostracize

To me, one of the most painful parts of Melvin's story occurred when he was removed from ministry, and the leaders of the church told him that no one in his congregation, and no fellow clergy, were to have contact with him. He was utterly ostracized.

In contrast to this type of response, the apostle Paul wrote, "Be kindly affectionate to one another with brotherly love, in honor giving preference to one another; not lagging in diligence, fervent in spirit, serving the Lord; rejoicing in hope, patient in tribulation, continuing steadfastly in prayer; distributing to the

needs of the saints, given to hospitality" (Romans 12:10–13 NKJV).
We are called to *give preference* to one another in love!

Why are we so afraid of those who fail? Are we fearful that
they will taint our own good reputation? Are we fearful that
similar failures in us might be exposed?

How do we dare say we know better than God who is worthy
of love and who isn't!

If we truly love God, we must recognize that God asks
us to show His love to others, and that means to love our
fellow Christians and non-Christians at every opportunity we
are given.

The Mantra of Our Love Revolution

I am increasingly convinced that loving others unconditionally
can make us think at times that we have lost our mind. We can
easily find ourselves asking, "Why would any sane person want
to do this?" Let's face it: there truly is little rationale for *why* we
are to love everyone, and no logical reason to explain why love is
so effective in changing lives!

Most of ministry is crisis oriented. People are lost—they need
to be found! People are struggling—they need to be rescued!
People are hungry—they need to be fed! People are homeless or
jobless—they need to be given shelter and jobs!

Ministry often involves perpetual storms of crisis. And it
takes a person who truly believes that God can and will provide,
protect, and be present to lead effectively.

I agree fully with Martin Luther King Jr., who said:

There are some things in our society, some things in our world, to which we should never be adjusted. There are some things concerning which we must always be maladjusted if we are to be people of good will. We must never adjust ourselves to racial discrimination and racial segregation. We must never adjust ourselves to religious bigotry. We must never adjust ourselves to economic conditions that take necessities from the many to give luxuries to the few. We must never adjust ourselves to the madness of militarism, and the self-defeating effects of physical violence.[1]

We are called to care deeply, love unconditionally, and be willing to work tirelessly to end racial discrimination, religious bigotry, and economic inequality.

In fact, we will not only *respond* in love, but we will *persevere* in love. That is our commitment to God and to others. When love perseveres, God is always there to accept it and give it back.

The mantra of our Love Revolution will be that our love . . .

Trusts God always,
Always looks for the best,
Never looks back,
But keeps going to the end. (1 Corinthians 13:7)

It's all about *love. Period.*

Responding . . .

1. The Love Revolution Manifesto at St. John's is our guiding principle. It says:

   > I will not be part of an institution or religion that judges or marginalizes a person based on race, abilities, gender, orientation, identity, or social status . . . but I will be a part of a Love Revolution that fights for the rights of people everywhere to love and be loved by God.

   What is your response to this manifesto?

2. Will you be a Love Revolutionary with me so that, together, we can change the world with *love—period*?

Notes

Chapter 2: Love Has No Conditions

1. John Dominic Crossan, *Jesus: A Revolutionary Biography* (New York: HarperOne, 2009), 105.

Chapter 3: Love Replaces Fear with Faith

1. Madeleine L'Engle, *Walking on Water: Reflections on Faith and Art* (Wheaton, IL: Harold Shaw, 1980), 190, 193.

2. Martin Luther King Jr. *Strength to Love* (Cleveland: Fortress Press, 1963), 117.

3. J. Keith Miller, *Compelled to Control: Recovering Intimacy in Broken Relationships* (Deerfield Beach, FL: Health Communications, 1997), 56.

4. Henri J. M. Nouwen, *The Dance of Life: Weaving Sorrows and Blessings into One Joyful Step,* ed. Michael Ford (Notre Dame: Ave Maria Press, 2005), 163–64.

5. C. S. Lewis, *The Problem of Pain* (New York: Collier, 1962), 93.

Chapter 4: Love Never Quits

1. Richard Rohr, *Hope against Darkness* (Cincinnati, OH: St. Anthony Messenger Press, 2001), 23.

Chapter 7: Love Honors Others

1. Robert Lupton, *Toxic Charity* (New York: HarperCollins, 2011), 14. Lupton cites a study reported in the March 18, 2008 issue of *USA Today.*

2. Ibid., 37.

3. Ibid., 16.

Chapter 9: Love Resists Anger

1. Robert S. McGee, *The Search for Significance: Seeing Your True Worth through God's Eyes*, rev. ed. (Nashville: Thomas Nelson, 2003), 31.
2. Derald Wing Sue, *Microagressions in Everyday Life: Race, Gender, and Sexual Orientation* (Hoboken, NJ: John Wiley and Sons, 2010), 66.

Conclusion: Moving Forward in Love

1. Martin Luther King Jr., "The Role of the Behavioral Scientist in the Civil Rights Movement," address delivered at the annual convention of the American Psychological Association, Washington, DC, September 1, 1967, http://www.apa.org/monitor/features/king-challenge.aspx.

About the Author

Pastor Rudy Rasmus has led St. John's United Methodist Church with his wife, Juanita, for more than twenty years. St. John's has grown to more than nine thousand members (three thousand of whom are, or were, homeless at one time) and is one of the most culturally diverse congregations in the country.

Pastor Rudy attributes the success of the church to a compassionate congregation that has embraced the vision of tearing down walls of classism, sexism, and racism, and replacing them with unconditional love and acceptance. Proud parents of two daughters, Rudy and Juanita live in Houston, Texas.

WORTHY
PUBLISHING

IF YOU ENJOYED THIS BOOK, WILL YOU CONSIDER SHARING THE MESSAGE WITH OTHERS?

- Mention the book in a Facebook post, Twitter update, Pinterest pin, or blog post.

- Recommend this book to those in your small group, book club, workplace, and classes.

- Head over to facebook.com/worthypublishing, "Like" the page, and post a comment as to what you enjoyed the most.

- Tweet "I recommend reading #LovePeriod by @PastorRudyR // @worthypub"

- Pick up a copy for someone you know who would be challenged and encouraged by this message.

- Write a book review online.

You can subscribe to Worthy Publishing's newsletter at worthypublishing.com.

WORTHY PUBLISHING
FACEBOOK PAGE

WORTHY PUBLISHING
WEBSITE